Let The Part Play You

A Practical Approach
To The
Actor's Creative Process

Fourth Edition, Revised

Anita Jesse

Wolf Creek Press

859 Hollywood Way, Suite 251
Burbank, CA 91505-2814

LET THE PART PLAY YOU (Fourth Edition, Revised)

Published by **Wolf Creek Press**
859 Hollywood Way, Suite 251
Burbank, CA 91505-2814
Phone: 818-767-4616
Fax: 818-767-2679
E-mail: WlfCrkPrs@aol.com

Manufactured in the United States of America

Publisher's Cataloging-in-Publication
(Provided by Quality Books, Inc)

Jesse, Anita.
    Let the part play you : a practical approach to the actor's
creative process / Anita Jesse. -- 4th ed., rev.
    p. cm.
    Includes bibliographical references and index.
    Preassigned LCCN: 97-61944
    ISBN: 0-9639655-2-2

    1. Acting.   I. Title.

PN2061.J47 1998   792'.028
                                   QBI97-41216

Acknowledgments

I want to thank my unselfish husband, Jim Ingersoll, for his help. Beginning with the earliest efforts to record these thoughts, he was there to support and inspire me and his invaluable criticism was essential. But, most of all, I thank him for tolerating me during the deadlines.

Thanks to my dear and fearless friend, Maureen McIntyre, who was there from the outset to provide heart, resources and insightful suggestions. Reenie's generosity is a constant source of amazement to me.

One of my great blessings has been my working relationship with Carol Woodliff. Carol has edited this edition of *Let The Part Play You* as well as, the recently published, *The Playing Is The Thing*. She is one of those exceptional people who knows how to offer criticism and suggestions in a manner that inspires you to keep digging for the best you have to offer. She generously took time from her own writing projects to hold my hand through this effort and keep me on track. She was so much more than an editor. She was a teacher, a friend, a cheerleader, and a magician. She was never fazed by the challenges and never found a problem too difficult to tackle. She is a talented writer—I hope I am fortunate enough to catch her between projects the next time I have a book to edit. And besides all that, she knows where to put the commas!

Over the last year, work in my office has been chaotic and taxing thanks to my efforts on this project. My sincere appreciation to Candy Belzer who has expertly navigated the confusion and helped free me to deal with my writing. Her loyalty, resourcefulness, and gentle spirit were more important than she will ever know.

During the final stages of preparation of this book, I had help from a superb team. I shudder to think of the workload had I been without their assistance. My thanks to: Earl Dittebrandt, Nick Granoski, Claudia Laslie and Tommy Woelfel.

Thanks to Lou Ida Marsh and Dr. James R. Miller who helped launch the book. They enthusiastically took me under their wings and I will always be grateful.

Judy Kerr has been an ardent supporter, a wellspring of information, and helped me believe it could be done. Thank you, Judy.

Thanks to Jim Fox for his continuing support. I will always be grateful to him for offering free advice to a total stranger when I first entertained the idea of writing a book. He is a man of great patience and charity.

Each edition of this book has involved a different group of experts making invaluable contributions. For the third edition, Adrienne Parsons served as able editor and furnished steady moral support as well as uncommon forbearance. I am still indebted to those who contributed to the first edition. Newell Alexander cheerfully invested many hours helping me and Ruth Richards waded through the earliest drafts with unflagging enthusiasm.

While I have been teaching long enough to have developed some strong opinions about how to communicate with actors, I don't claim to have devised an original method of working. I only hope I have articulated my approach in a way that makes it accessible and practical. Like any teacher, I owe an enormous debt to all the instructors with whom I have studied as well as to the teachers who have generously shared their methods in excellent books. I salute Dr. Francis Hodge whose wisdom I appreciate more every day. Like most students, I didn't comprehend the value of his instruction while I labored under his demanding supervision. There are two other teachers I want to acknowledge, but my methods are so far afield by now from the methods they espouse, I feel I should issue a disclaimer *for them* before I mention them. I hope they won't feel they have to take the blame for ideas they find foolish. My thanks to Brett Dunham and Laura Rose. The list of teachers and directors who have shared their insight and techniques in books and articles is long and I am grateful to be teaching in an age when these materials are so readily available.

Thank you, Mom, for never doubting me.

Finally, my deepest appreciation to all the actors I have worked with over the years for what they have taught me. Their passion for their work, their gratitude for guidance received, their dedication to their art, their faith in me—all these have sustained me. I have witnessed on a daily basis the uncommon spirit to be found in actors and because of the warmth of my relationship with these brave souls, I am blessed to have found a life's work that is challenging and fulfilling. I thank them for their contributions large and small to this project and for the encouragement they have so generously given me. Without them there would be no books. More importantly, without them my life would be the poorer.

Table of Contents

The actor should not play a part. Like the Aeolian harps that used to be hung in the trees to be played only by the breeze, the actor should be an instrument played upon by the character he depicts.

Alla Nazimova, quoted in *Actors On Acting*

FREEING THE ACTOR WITHIN

Work is love made visible. And if you cannot work with love but only with distaste, it is better that you should leave your work and sit at the gate of the temple and take alms of those who work with joy.

Kahlil Gibran, *The Prophet. On Work.*

Freeing The Actor Within

An ancient myth holds that inside the block of marble a form sleeps, waiting for the sculptor to strip away its marble confines. It is an allegory that will serve you well, I believe. For trapped inside the "marble confines" of your fears, doubts, and expectations is the artist within you. If you wish to become an accomplished actor, you must not only learn the techniques unique to your craft, you must free the creative being within you. Before we continue with this comparison, let me assure you that I am *not* promoting some romantic notion of spontaneous eruption of your talent. I am not encouraging you to merely dream of becoming an actor, then hope to awaken one morning and discover that the artist within has emerged overnight. If you were a sculptor, you wouldn't expect the form within the marble to get restless and escape one day. You would understand that you must free the form by diligently chipping away at the intractable rock.

Similarly, you will have to work at your craft to free the actor within. You must learn to effectively read a script, perceive character, and grasp the nuances of action. You must learn to control performance anxieties, use your emotions effectively, learn lines, and commit to the character's imaginary reality. There is also a long list of technical skills you must master, such as cheating to camera and creating intimacy on stage while projecting your voice to fill an auditorium. But almost any proficient actor will tell you that expertise in all of these technical areas depends on a short list of basic skills. **Those building blocks are concentration, imagination, access to emotions, listening, observation, and relaxation.** These are the rudiments of your craft, and you will have to master them if you hope to become expert in the more technical areas. While absolute mastery of these skills is no easy task, you enjoy a distinct advantage. You have already started the work. You established the foundation of your craft long ago when you began to develop these skills as a child.

Look once again at that list of building-block skills. You were born with the ability to concentrate. You have used your imagination since you were a child. Your emotional capacity is basic equipment. You listen and respond, at least to some extent, every day of your life. You act and react every moment you are awake. You came into the world with an innate gift for mimicry. You easily memorized nursery rhymes, or song lyrics, as a child long before you knew memorizing was a valuable skill.

It's true that acting is more complicated than natural mimicry and memorizing nursery rhymes. Rest assured, I'm not implying that anybody can be a great actor or that reading this book will make you a skilled performer. Becoming a proficient actor isn't necessarily easy—even though the performance itself should always *look* effortless. But, because the skills that form the basis for your craft are not foreign to you, developing your craft has more to do with restoring and refining familiar, but underused, skills than with acquiring new and alien ones. After all, the actor whose ego has become overly inflated is apt to be brought back to earth with a reminder from a fellow performer that "This isn't brain surgery." When quizzed about her craft, academy award winner, Sissy Spacek once replied—with tongue firmly planted in cheek, "Listen, if it was easy, women and children would be doin' it."[1]

This Old House

Since a major part of your work will be reclaiming and refining skills you already have, another way to look at this process is to compare learning to act with renovating an old house. In other words, rather than creating a new structure, you will remodel an existing one. If that statement prompts you to think you have an easy task ahead of you, perhaps you don't know much about construction. Those who have building experience know that in some ways restoration is the more nerve-racking project. You will spend hours tearing down old walls so you can build new ones. There will be times when you curse the old treasure you fell in love with, wishing you could ditch the monstrosity and start from scratch. You have fantasies that include TNT.

Here's the rub: as a potential homeowner you can choose either to restore an old house, or build a new one—as an actor you don't have a choice. You are stuck with tearing down walls and pulling out rotten flooring. You even have to live in the *house* while you do the work. The advantage of remodeling the old house is that you begin with a foundation and a basic structure. The downside is that the elements of that basic structure which don't suit your current needs will require alterations and those alterations may end up being more time-consuming and costly than new construction. You can expect some major headaches. Similarly, your reclamation of the actor within is sure to be a long and uneven process. If you succeed in freeing the actor buried under years of counter-productive habits, it will almost certainly be because you devoted countless hours to the renovation. Sometimes it will be painful, exhausting and heartbreaking work. Sometimes it will be a joyful celebration of spirit. It will always take discipline, perseverance, patience and a burning desire.

A Sure-Fire Investment

This is the encouraging news: the energy devoted to this reclamation is one of life's rare sure-fire investments. I call it a sure thing because, as an actor, you need basic competence in certain areas to provide the foundation for your craft. Coincidentally, those same skills are essential life-skills. Exceptional actors have polished the techniques of their specific craft; but, first, they excelled in concentration, imagination, listening, access to emotional life, observation, and relaxation. Examine these areas individually and notice that the more capable you are in each of them the richer your life will be.

Concentration is the foundational skill that supports all learning, whether it be on stage, on the tennis court, at the computer, or in the classroom. When you can focus your attention and screen out distractions—including the voice of your inner critic, you are free to channel your energies into the task at hand. Strengthening your imagination enhances your problem-solving abilities and paves the way for success in all creative endeavors. How could you lose by establishing a better connection with your emotions, thereby making it possible to bring more of yourself to every enterprise? What about listening skills? Good listeners are more effective communicators. Even people who seldom communicate with others in their work need this skill for personal relationships. Your powers of observation allow you to learn from what is going on around you. Knowing how to relax, how to relieve paralyzing tension, will clearly help you cope with the stress of contemporary life. Last but not least, while you master the basics of the actor's craft, you will gain a deeper appreciation for the performances you see on stage and screen.

So, if your mastery of these skills helps you to become a polished actor and you have a successful career, you win big. If, instead, you move on to other interests, you still win. You win because the tools you have acquired will provide a foundation for excellence in whatever fields you pursue. Make the investment. There aren't many sure-fire bets around.

THE KEY TO CONFIDENCE IS A TECHNIQUE THAT WORKS

The theory behind *Let The Part Play You* is that you hone basic skills, then you learn to utilize those skills to set free the artist within you. The awakening, refining and refocusing of your basic human skills provides the foundation for your technique. Then, building on this solid foundation, you can master the basics of your craft. That mastery allows you to *let go* and become an "instrument played upon" by whatever character you depict. Since the third edition of this book was published, I have written a companion book, *The Playing Is The Thing*. I hope you will refer to that book for additional source material as you seek to master the basic skills. Both books provide instruction that can help smooth the path you travel during your journey of self-discovery.

You won't find any hocus-pocus in the following chapters—any fast-acting, hot-off-the-press secrets. Just as every novice actor hopes there is a blueprint for a successful career in this business, everyone dreams of a foolproof technique or *method* for the mastery of the craft. There are no infallible formulas for either. Acting is an art, not a science. Moreover, each actor is unique in emotional make-up, life experience and prior training. To further confuse the novice, many professional actors claim to have *no* system or method of working—they will tell you they "just do it." (The truth is these actors prepare on an unconscious level and are unable or unwilling to articulate their process.)

What you will find in these pages are some dependable tools and an approach that has, for many actors, for many years, demystified the process. Some of these techniques will work for you from the beginning; some will take weeks of arduous repetition to make a difference; and others simply may never work for you. It's a trial-and-error process. Ultimately you must devise your own method based on all the information you can scrounge from every available source.

LEARNING TO LET GO

My chief goal is to persuade you that, regardless of what methods of preparation you use, the intent should be to free you of doubts and fears, as well as awaken your unconscious to possibilities. The energy you invest in preparation should provide a springboard that will thrust you, as the character, into an exploration of dramatic action. It shouldn't give you, as the actor, more to worry about or live up to. Alla Nazimova, the celebrated Russian actor whose portrayals of Ibsen's women in the first part of the twentieth century were heralded as definitive, said it elegantly:

> The actor should not play a part. Like the Aeolian harps that
> used to be hung in the trees to be played only by the breeze,
> the actor should be an instrument played upon by the character he depicts.[2]

No one can *teach* you to be an actor—that must be left to the creative spirit within you. I hope you will become the finest actor you can possibly be. I hope you will bring authenticity to your work and become the kind of actor who reveals your unique quality in a way that continually surprises your audience and illuminates the character you portray as no other human being could. I hope you will discover, or rediscover, the joy in acting. (At least in the beginning, it must have been something you did because it was pleasurable.) I want you to experience, regularly, the incomparable satisfaction that results from the creative act.

On your way to mastering your craft, I hope you will acquire a deeper appreciation for this remarkable process by which an actor brings a character to life. I continually delight in the sleights of hand that actors perform. Thanks to imagination and craft, an actor can transform into a person who has never before existed—not just an *interpretation* of a character, but a fully-dimensional human being with a soul and a heart, with humor and pain and love and loss. Your skills, when fully developed, will permit you to endow an imaginary being with a human form. This is truly the most profound kind of magic.

> For acting is a process of incarnation. Just that. And it is a
> miracle. I have no words to express what I feel about this
> subtle, ancient, sacred art—the marvel of it, the wonder, the
> meaning.[3]

The creative process can be a means of discovering a voice for the you inside you—the tender, secret you—that has long been buried within the rubble of expectations. May it be so for you.

FOOTNOTES

[1]Sissy Spacek, quoted by Pat Dowell, "Mettle Of The Belle," *American Film*, March 1991, p. 29.
[2]Alla Nazimova, quoted by Morton Eustis, *Players at Work; Acting According to the Actors* (New York: Theatre Arts, 1937) pp. 51-58 passim. Copyright 1937. Quoted in *Actors On Acting* ed. by Toby Cole and Helen Krich Chinoy (New York: Crown Publishers, 1970) p. 590. Copyright Cole and Chinoy, 1970.
[3]Robert Edmond Jones, *The Dramatic Imagination* (New York: Theatre Arts Books, 1965) p. 31. Copyright Robert Edmond Jones, 1941.

You are curled up on the most comfortable over-stuffed chair in your living room reading your favorite author's latest book. You are devouring the next to last chapter; the action is building to the climax; the suspense is delicious. *Will she, or won't she?* The air conditioner runs in the background; you don't hear it. *Can he, or can't he?* Someone across the street starts a car; you aren't aware of it. *Did they, or didn't they?* The dog down the street was barking a minute ago; you didn't notice.

How much force were you exerting to keep your attention on your book? It seemed effortless, right?

CHAPTER 1

LEARNING TO CONCENTRATE

Purple Giraffes

In mastering the art of concentration, you are developing an essential life-skill. Anyone who aspires to success—be it as a baseball player, heart surgeon, stock broker, or violinist—must develop strong powers of concentration. Until you master this skill, you will be, at worst, a mediocre actor whose work is never quite up to par or at best, an inconsistent actor whose work varies wildly from riveting to embarrassing.

Until you can focus your attention with pin-point accuracy—screening out all distractions, acting and preparing to act will be difficult and frustrating. If your mind wanders aimlessly, you will struggle unsuccessfully with everything from studying the script and rehearsing to hearing the comments on your work after the performance. You may find, for example, that although you settle down with the best of intentions to investigate your part, your mind keeps wandering to whether you will play the role effectively. Perhaps you have set aside time to learn lines, but you find yourself, instead, agonizing over unpaid bills or fantasizing about a vacation. The last time you were on stage, or in front of the camera, you may have had trouble screening out anxious thoughts about the effectiveness of your performance. Have you recently forgotten your lines on stage? Has a director or teacher told you lately that you weren't *in character*, or that you weren't listening, or that you weren't playing the action? If any of these problems sound familiar, you should begin working immediately to improve your concentration.

LEARNING TO SWITCH ON CONCENTRATION

Concentration may be defined as the direction of one's attention to a selected object or subject. Your mind focuses on one target. That target fills the foreground while everything else fades into background. Unless you either consciously or unconsciously select a foreground, your mind will roam aimlessly from one thing to another. One minute you are thinking about the scene you are going to play tomorrow; the next moment you may drift to a daydream about your love life. You may even believe you are thinking about more than one thing at a time. What you are doing, however, is rapidly shifting your attention back and forth between the objects of concentration—you are capable of changing your mental target as frequently as twice per second.

It is possible to transfer extremely complicated tasks to what is often called the *automatic mind*. In such cases, you learn the skill and practice it until you can pursue the activity without consciously paying attention to it. This shifting of tasks to the automatic mind is something you have been doing since you were a child. When you learned to ride a bicycle or drive a car, those skills seemed overwhelmingly complex. You couldn't possibly think about anything else while you were struggling to keep your balance on two wheels, or coordinate clutch and brake. Now while you ride that bicycle, you talk to a friend riding beside you, watch the traffic, and still have time to notice pretty girls or good-looking guys. Activities that once required all your attention have been given over to the automatic mind. In traffic, whether on your bicycle or driving your car, you are peripherally aware of staying upright or shifting gears. But your center of concentration is—we hope—cars in front of you, cars coming at you, pedestrians, and traffic lights.

Sometimes you consciously order your mind to focus on a particular mental target, then struggle to screen out distractions. Other times it's almost as if the mental target chooses you, and everything else seems to automatically fade from awareness. **Without being conscious of the moment you "switch on" your concentration, you become engrossed in the things that interest you.** You will effortlessly become enthralled by an appealing movie or book, a person you find attractive, your favorite music, an intriguing puzzle, a conversation that excites you. It's almost as if you have *unconsciously* hit the switch that focuses attention on a particular object or train of thought.

Experts in every field know exactly how to find the switch that activates concentration. They don't wait for a mental target to emerge from the background. They can select a point of concentration and hold that object, or train of thought, in the forefront of consciousness while screening out distractions. As an actor, you must consistently find that switch and you must be capable of becoming preoccupied with what may not automatically interest you. You cannot be at the mercy of your wandering mind. You must:

1. **Identify the appropriate mental target.**
2. **Practice basic actor skills until you can relegate them to the automatic mind.**

3. Train your mind to hold the mental target of your choice at the center of your awareness, regardless of distractions.

Identifying The Target

If you are a tennis player, your intention, or goal, is to get the ball over the net and out of your opponent's reach; therefore, your immediate point of concentration is the ball. You have probably heard athletes talk about that kind of concentration. When a baseball player's batting average is improving, he may say, "I've been seeing the ball better lately."

You may believe that, during performance, you have to keep yourself and your work at the center of your awareness. Perhaps you assume that you should monitor your performance to guarantee that it pleases the director. You may think you have to satisfy the writer, a fellow actor, a critic, or the audience, in general. If you subscribe to any of these theories, you probably have concluded that an actor's mental targets should be actor concerns such as: emotions, stage business, posture, remembering lines, voice production, or audience response. This assumption may seem logical, particularly since people who comment on your work will frequently mention those matters. Actually, while playing a role, neither actor jobs nor any other of your personal concerns should occupy the center of your awareness. You should be *in character*, which means **the character's problems and the need to solve those problems should be at the center of your awareness. Your actor-needs shift to the periphery of your awareness**.

Suppose you are playing a character who wants to thank her mother for being there when times were difficult. Begin by setting aside your actor-concerns so you can commit all your physical and mental powers to satisfying the character's needs. Once you fully commit to communicating your gratitude to your mother, you will inevitably direct your attention away from yourself. You will turn your attention toward the responses of the character playing your mother because only your mother's reactions can tell you whether or not you are accomplishing your objective. After all, if you ignore the other character and scrutinize your actions, you won't be able to effectively judge your progress. You may think you need to keep track of how well you are doing the thanking, but this tactic will cause you to miss the essential information. Because you are distracted, you won't realize that you aren't getting through—you won't learn that you aren't successfully conveying your appreciation. You won't discover that you have to change your strategy.

The audience cares about what happens to the character. They do not want to be reminded constantly of the actor. If your attention is on yourself, you reveal the actor playing the role and almost nothing about the character or what is happening in the scene. Identifying the appropriate mental target enables you to make the transition from amateurish work to memorable performances. There is much more to come on this subject in Chapters 8 and 14.

Trusting The Automatic Mind

To the novice, it seems logical to choose as your mental targets the long list of actor jobs. Surely, the beginner thinks, the bulk of attention belongs on: hitting marks, projecting the voice, making crosses, using props, finding the light, remembering lines, and waiting for laughs. After all, they clearly are part of your job description. Without a doubt, you must make your cross, pick up your prop, find your light, and project your voice. These duties, however, must be relegated to the automatic mind when you are playing your role. They must not be at the center of your concentration. The object or train of thought that is at the character's center of awareness must be your mental target. If your character is thinking about learning another character's secret, then the center of your awareness must be reserved for the mystery, not your actor responsibilities. Many actors distrust this instruction. After all, they know from experience that the more complex a task is the more selective and effective concentration must be. Why then, when you are acting, shouldn't you pay attention to such tasks as hitting marks and remembering dialogue? The actor who is afraid to take his attention off actor duties is forgetting that after we learn to perform complicated tasks we typically shift those jobs to the automatic mind. In other words, our body learns the skills. This is why you can drive a car, or ride a bicycle, without consciously thinking about it.

You should not automatically assume you will know your lines or remember your blocking. Only hours invested in concentrated practice of basic acting skills (such as projection) and rehearsal of those specific moves (such as handling the props) will allow you to entrust those assignments to the automatic mind. Actors who don't invest time perfecting the basic skills do sloppy and unprofessional work. But actors who acquire the skills, then fail to trust the automatic mind, haven't a prayer of getting into character. If hitting your mark occupies the center of your awareness while you are playing your scene, you aren't *in* the scene—you are just an actor hitting marks. Acting teachers and directors are fond of telling actors to trust. The capacity of the automatic mind is one thing you can trust.

The Keys To Mastery

Through exercises and constant practice, you can learn to control the focus of your attention as effectively as you control the beam of a flashlight. You have the capacity to select a subject and hold that subject at the center of your awareness regardless of distractions. Stanislavski told his students the story of a Maharajah who, in order to select a minister worthy of the post, applied a test. Each candidate was handed a dish full to the brim with milk and told to walk around on top of the city walls. The man who didn't spill a drop of the liquid was to be appointed to office. Several applicants attempted the task, but when distracted by the yelling or jeering of the crowd, they each spilled the milk. Finally, there came a man who could not be distracted by the screams, threats, or jeers. The commander of the troops yelled, "Fire!" but when the troops fired, the man's hands remained steady and no milk was spilled.

"I have found my minister," said the Maharajah. Then he turned to the man and asked, "Didn't you hear the crowd cry out at you?"

"No."

"Didn't you hear the shots?"

"No," answered the new minister, "I was watching the milk."[1]

There are four keys to acquiring such masterful concentration:

* **Concentration follows interest.**

- **You must silence your inner critic.**
- **Your mind will respond best to gentle direction.**
- **Practice makes perfect.**

CONCENTRATION FOLLOWS INTEREST

The primary secret to mastering the art of concentration is making certain your mental target interests you enough to hold your attention. All your life your attention has gravitated toward those things that interested you, and never has effective concentration had anything to do with Herculean effort and excessive tension. You can't command yourself to concentrate any more than you could make yourself fall asleep. Indeed, if you struggle to concentrate, you are not focusing on your mental target—you are focusing on yourself and your imagined inability to concentrate. You are concentrating on concentrating. You don't need to learn *how* to concentrate. Instead, you need to learn how to direct your attention to *the object of your choice*, and how to create sufficient interest in the target to keep your attention there. You may not automatically become engrossed in someone else's needs, problems, dreams, and fears; however, that is exactly what acting is all about. You must learn to make what interests you, the character, more absorbing than what interests you, the actor.

Don't focus on distractions. The more you try not to think about a pink elephant with wonderful floppy ears and painted toenails, the bigger and pinker he becomes. If you want to fill the center of your awareness with something other than the pink elephant, you must choose a mental target, then endow that target with qualities that make it even more fascinating than the elephant. Suppose you want to make a giraffe your mental target. Try painting him a vibrant purple, then splash him with huge green polka-dots, and, finally, furnish him with a big goofy smile and enormous eyes looking straight at you. Soon there is no room in the circle of your awareness for the pink elephant.

What if you are playing a scene in which you, the character, need information that another character can supply? Provided you have mastered concentration, you will recall how you plan to use the information and what will happen if you can't learn the facts. You will become preoccupied with the desire to get the information from the other character and you are likely to dedicate your mental and physical energies to this enterprise. If, however, you are still struggling with your concentration, you will be distracted by your actor-need to play the scene successfully. If so distracted, you must find a way to redirect your attention to your character-needs. In other words, your actor-needs will be the pink elephant—growing larger and more demanding as you struggle to ignore them. You must manage to make the character's needs (the giraffe) more interesting, more colorful, more urgent, more demanding than your actor-needs (the pink elephant.)

THE DOER AND THE CRITIC

The doer performs; the critic comments on the performance. Like most actors, you probably have a critic inside you who wants to chatter almost non-stop about your work—issuing questions, demands, criticisms, punishments, and threats. Very likely, you think you can't survive without this self-talk; however, the judging, worrying and blaming only serve to insulate you from any interchange with others. In one of his excellent books,

Timothy Gallwey says, "Be clear about this: letting go of judgments does not mean ignoring errors. It simply means seeing events as they are and not adding anything to them."[2] You must learn to silence the critic and trust the doer.

You can silence the self-talk only when you learn to trust your abilities and when the desire to reveal the character is greater than your need to evaluate your performance. In other words, you can play the scene without side-coaching from your inner critic when you meet these goals. (1) You know that you are as prepared as possible. (2) Your obligation to the character's goals is greater than your obligation to your actor-needs. Resist the temptation to watch your performance even when your inner critic insists that the only way you can guarantee commendable work is to monitor yourself. Learn to love doing the work more than you love watching yourself do it.

A Carrot Works Better Than A Stick

Punishing yourself for the internal chatter will simply make matters worse. Unless you have chosen a mental target that fully engages your interest, your attention inevitably will gravitate *away* from your selected target *to* whatever you automatically find fascinating. The loss of concentration is frustrating, but if you take time to chastise yourself when this happens, you are changing the focal point of your attention. At that point, you have made your concentration skills the target of your attention. Scolding yourself is a waste of energy, and it makes you increasingly self-conscious. Instead, each time your mind wanders from the target—and it definitely will wander—gently redirect your attention to the subject you have chosen.

Practice Makes Perfect

Students tend to skim over the exercises in books. The thought process goes something like this: "Oh, yeah, yeah, I'll come back to these later, but now I want to get to the important stuff." Let me tell you: this *is* the important stuff. Until you can focus your mind at will, you cannot stay in character, and until you can stay in character, you are not a proficient actor. This book is designed as a workbook, or manual, and if you do not *work* your way through the material you are wasting a resource. Merely reading the exercises will do you little good—just as reading about a new diet will not cause weight loss. Only *applying* these exercises will make a difference.

EXERCISES

Keep these guidelines in mind as you practice the exercises:

☛ **Be kind to yourself.**
Your mind will respond best to gentle self-direction. If you beat up on yourself when your attention wanders, you won't make progress; indeed, you may make matters worse.

☞ **You don't get a hit unless you swing the bat.**
Mistakes let us know what not to do next time, rather than how worthless we are. It's no coincidence that Babe Ruth, who once had the most home runs on record, struck out 1,331 times.[3]

☞ **Make the exercises fun.**
Turn the exercises into games. If you think of them as work, you simply won't do them as often.

☞ **Remember the Swiss cheese.**
Apply the Swiss cheese theory to all your exercise sessions—nibble away at the work. Since you will have a million excuses for not doing the exercises, promise yourself to play a concentration game for no longer than two minutes. Set a timer and when the time is up, stop if you need to. You're better off working only two minutes every day than you are playing catch-up for half an hour every two weeks.

☞ **Reclaim a skill.**
You already know how to do this. At this point, you are acquiring mastery of a skill you have used haphazardly all your life.

☞ **Use your time wisely.**
"Doing My Job," "I'd Rather Not," and "Sensory Hopscotch" will enable you to improve concentration skills without reserving time for exercises. Economize.

Doing My Job

While on the freeway, make driving the center of your concentration. That means that each time your mind wanders, you refocus. When your attention drifts to what you will do when you get to your destination, begins replays of past events, or strays to the day's to-do list, you gently redirect your attention to this moment—to what is happening right now. Focus on the cars in front of you, the cars behind you, the feel of your car, everything happening on the road and exactly how it relates to you. Use variations of this exercise in all your activities—reading, eating, talking to a friend, washing dishes. When you learn to focus your mind, you will be amazed at how restful it is to quiet the chatter of your internal critic. (For additional help with this exercise, read a Timothy Gallwey book and Lawrence LeShan's *How to Meditate*. Check the "Suggested Reading List" for more information.)

Double Talk

Turn on the television and the radio. Find two talk shows and adjust both programs at equal volume level. Set a timer for one minute. Concentrate on the radio show for one minute, then concentrate on the television program for one minute. After switching back and forth a couple of times, stop and write notes on what you have heard.

Cross-Fire

Turn on your favorite TV show. Now, in spite of the distraction, carry out a demanding mental task—memorize a poem or solve a mathematical problem.

I'd Rather Not

Tackle a job you have been postponing (paying bills, memorizing a monologue, or organizing income tax information) and devote yourself to that task for a set period. For example, promise yourself that you will work at this task for no longer than ten minutes. Set a timer. Resolve that the second the timer goes off, you will return to what genuinely interests you. Don't be surprised if you find yourself, at the end of the time limit, engrossed in what was a dreaded assignment. To make the exercise more challenging, stop whatever you are doing when the timer goes off and return to what interested you before you began the exercise.

Sensory Hopscotch

Switch your attention from one type of sensory information to another. For instance, if you are sitting in front of the TV, presumably you are focusing on seeing and hearing. Switch your attention to the tactile sense (your bottom on the chair, the clothes on your body, the temperature in the room.) You should be able to come up with several variations based on this exercise.

Under Fire

Perform a monologue while besieged by distractions. Stay in character and say your lines even though a friend tries to get your attention by talking to you, waving his arms, or making funny faces.

Your mind is not a helpless, empty vessel waiting to be filled by whatever happens to be hovering around you. With practice, you can learn to choose a mental target, place it at the center of your awareness, and hold it there regardless of distractions. Script exploration, remembering lines, audition pressures—all these become manageable only if you master concentration. This is the bedrock upon which you will build all your other acting skills.

FOOTNOTES

[1]Constantin Stanislavski, *An Actor Prepares* (New York: Theatre Arts Books, 1963) p. 81. Copyright Elizabeth R. Hapgood, 1948.
[2]W. Timothy Gallwey, *The Inner Game of Tennis* (New York: Random House, 1974) p. 36.
[3]Paul A. Hauck, *Overcoming Worry and Fear* (Philadelphia: The Westminster Press, 1975) p. 88.

That minister of ministers,
Imagination, gathers up
The undiscovered Universe
Like jewels in a jasper cup.
John Davidson,
There Is a Dish to
Hold the Sea

CHAPTER 2

DEVELOPING YOUR IMAGINATION

Cowboys And Indians

Ultimately acting is playing cowboys and Indians. Children instinctively commit themselves physically, mentally and emotionally to the components of an imaginary reality. Effortlessly, they imagine the specifics of their character's world, then eagerly behave as if they occupied that world. Acting involves the same process. Essentially it is "let's play like ...." You can infuse a character with a life force only if you are willing to embrace the simple techniques used by the child who "becomes" a cowboy, a princess, a firefighter, a race car driver, or a ballerina. Imagination allows you to become more fascinated by the problems and obstacles in the imaginary reality of the character's world than you are with the challenges in the actual reality of your own actor's world. **The essence of acting is *make-believe.***

Stanislavski taught his actors to use the "magic *if*"—in other words to think and behave, in performance, *as if* they were the characters, and *as if* the given circumstances were real. In the imaginary reality of the scene, the other actor becomes whatever the writer has dictated—your lover/parent/friend/enemy/brother/sister—and you behave *as if* that were true. While playing, you fasten all your attention on your character's problems *as if* they were your real-life problems and you commit all your energies to finding solutions. If you cannot make that leap of faith, how could you expect the audience to do it? Alla Nazimova, the Russian actor mentioned in the previous chapter, put imagination in perspective. She said: "First, last and always, a player must have imagination. Without imagination, he might as well be a shoe-black as an actor."[1]

Two Types Of Imagination

According to the *American College Dictionary*, imagination is "the action of forming mental images or concepts of what is not actually present to the senses." Those images include some, or all, of the senses: sight, sound, touch, smell and taste. One sense may trigger a series of images eventually involving all the senses. One whiff of a familiar perfume can produce a flood of sensory images from your past—the melody of a song, the texture of a dress, the heat of a crowded room, the light reflecting off the mirrored ball overhead. Countless images are stored in the memory and, under the suggestion of a similar or associated image, the original image is evoked. For example, if you grew up in a family where the evening meal was a convivial occasion, the mention of "dinner" will fill your mind with images of people talking, laughing, hugging, and proposing toasts. This process is called *reproductive imagination*.

When you use your *creative imagination*, you recombine images from previous experiences to form mental pictures that are different from any in your actual experience. Let's say you are to play someone who grew up in a family where dinner was a cold, formal function. Since the images from your own past are inappropriate, you will draw mental pictures from personal and vicarious experiences and then use your creative imagination to recombine those images. With this creative faculty you can produce vivid images of stoic faces across the table, the loud ticking of the grandfather clock, stiff backs plastered against hard chairs, and people staring at their plates.

While you will use both reproductive and creative imagination in your work, clearly, it is the creative form that permits you to play a wider range of roles. The successful novelist Irving Wallace declares: "You were provided with imagination. Use it. Da Vinci did not have to attend the Last Supper to paint it."[2]

Your Imagination Is A Workhorse

It is easy to recognize the part concentration plays in the success of the baseball pitcher, scientist, jet pilot, and violinist. Imagination plays an equally fundamental role. Whatever our ambitions, it is our ability to *see* ourselves overcoming obstacles that inspires us to persevere. Without that mental picture of success, the struggling young musician or ballplayer probably would not have persisted through all those classes, assignments, or practice sessions.

Like concentration, imagination is a faculty everyone possesses. People who think they have no creative abilities readily imagine themselves relaxing at the beach while they are, in truth, slugging it out on the freeway in rush hour traffic. Furthermore, if our freeway driver is a job applicant on the way to an interview, the person probably easily summons a *vision* of what will happen in the prospective employer's office. With no special training, the prospective employee conjures up a deliciously clear mental picture of the potential employer saying "yes" to the carefully rehearsed presentation. If our hero is a pessimist, the employer probably says "no." All of us have *seen* the person we love with someone else, or a loved one being harmed, or ourselves winning a prize. The actor who agonizes over a lack of imagination will effortlessly create vivid images of a humiliating performance.

There is no doubt that you have imagination. The pertinent questions are:

- Do you know how to make it work for you?
- Do you use it frequently enough to have confidence in it?
- When you exercise your imagination, is it because you made a conscious decision to do so?

Use It Or Lose It

You will regularly summon your imagination in all phases of your work. You will need to consciously call up stored images, or recombine old experiences thereby creating new representations. Like concentration, imagination is a powerful *muscle* that must be exercised and toned if you expect to use it effectively. Even if you don't aspire to stardom, everyday living is a creative process and you need a powerful imagination to cope successfully. The most prosaic forms of problem solving require use of your imagination. When faced with one of life's stumbling blocks, you must examine the obstacle, then "make up" a solution that, at first, exists only in your mind's eye. This process of visualization—recombining images into something different from your actual experience—is the key to creativity, in any form. When you strengthen your imagination, you develop a vital life-skill.

EXERCISES

Keep these guidelines in mind as you play these games:

☛ **You know how to daydream—you are strengthening an innate, but possibly underused, skill.**
You are not learning how to imagine; you already daydream, imagining events as you wish they had evolved, and fantasize about your future. You are training yourself to image when you choose to do so, and you are developing an imagination that is even more vivid and less limited by reality.

☛ **Be gentle with yourself.**
You may have to coax your imagination to "come out and play." If, as a child, you were criticized for daydreaming and constantly made to feel foolish for taking flights of fancy, you must retrain your mind. You will need patience and practice. If you find it difficult to conceive of yourself in circumstances radically different from your own, try starting with small stretches. Place yourself in an imaginary situation only slightly unlike your reality. If your logical mind balks, retreat to a scenario that is

nearer to the truth, then venture out again. Be as loving and gentle as you would be with a shy child.

☞ **Make time.**

Exercise your imagination throughout the day, every day. If you think you don't have time, be creative. Following these guidelines, you will find games you can play while doing your everyday chores. Combine imagination exercises with your concentration games. Begin immediately utilizing your new skills during your preparation for a role.

☞ **Use all your senses.**

See, hear, smell, touch and taste all the elements of your daydreams. Don't rush. Savor the details.

☞ **Don't go for the emotional response.**

Much of this work will stir your feelings—that's normal. However, that must not be your goal. Although you shouldn't inhibit your emotions, stay focused on the details of the exercise and don't fall in love with your feelings. Don't try to recapture particular emotions. Focus on the action of the imaginary event—what you are doing and what is being done to you. If you direct your imagination to create a state of doing, you can trust that the actions will produce emotional responses.

☞ **Have fun.**

If you view this process of developing your imagination as drudgery, you obviously won't spend much time on it. This is what you did for fun when you were a child. Rediscover that joy. Daydream pleasant scenarios. Drift off into fantasies about playing a favorite role then basking in the kudos at the curtain call. Remember a pleasant occasion. Allow the memories to fill you with a glow of well-being. After you have found confidence in your ability to use your imagination, you can venture into whatever daydreams are appropriate for your character—whether they are pleasant or unpleasant.

> ## REMEMBER WHEN

Create an imaginary memory for yourself. *Remember when* your older brother came back from the war; or *remember when* your mother told you that your sister had left home to join the circus; or *remember when* you and your grandmother left to go to Europe for the summer. *Relive* the story of this imaginary event. You will find yourself using some actual events as well as some real people combined with people and events you don't recognize. Don't concern yourself with where this is going; just begin *living* it.

Be sure to concentrate on what you, and the other people, did—the physical actions. Be precise about the time of day, what you were wearing, what people said and did. Be specific about sensory experiences. Identify your body's temperature. Remember how your clothes felt against your skin—including the texture and weight. Recall the taste in your mouth; the nearby sounds and the distant ones; as well as the odors around you. Bring back the degree of relaxation and tension you felt in various parts of your body. Recall the colors and textures of objects that surrounded you.

Don't get sidetracked onto what you were feeling; let the emotions emerge out of the actions. Pay attention to the specifics. Heed the dictum of the architect, Ludwig Mies van der Rohe: "God is in the details."

Here is an example of a *remember when*:

(Find a quiet place and read the exercise. Allow yourself to see, hear, touch, taste and smell the described experiences. Don't rush. If you have unresolved grief over the death of a loved one, or even if you are simply an extremely emotional person, ask for some help with this specific *remember when*. Ask a trusted friend to provide emotional support if you need it.)

Remember the last time you visited your grandfather? Remember walking up the sidewalk and feeling the heat of the cement, even through your shoes? Your shirt is sticking to you because you're damp with perspiration and your shoes feel tight—the way they do on a hot, sticky day. The old scraggly dog next door is yapping at you as though he's never seen you before.

Climb the porch steps; hear the sound of the step that has always creaked and see the white paint, cracked with age. Feel the stored heat of the familiar screen door handle as you open the front door and step inside the living room. The first thing that hits you is the smell. Grandma and Grandpa's house always smelled like freshly laundered curtains, gingerbread cookies, and Christmas trees. Now the odors that assault your nose are sharp and medicinal—alcohol and bedpans. The living room is stuffy and the seldom closed curtains are drawn. It takes a few seconds for your eyes to adjust after the scorching light of the outdoors.

See your mother come into the living room from the back of the house. She has circles under her eyes. She wears house slippers and her hair has come down in back; she must have lost a couple of pins. She is wearing one of grandma's aprons—the pink checked one with the funny little bib and the big pocket on the left side bordered with a narrow ruffle.

Remember, that's the pocket where Grandma always kept the lemon drops. When your mother wasn't within earshot, Grandma would say, "Can you keep a secret?" Then she would slip you a lemon drop. But Grandpa would smell those lemon drops a mile away and he loved to tease Grandma, your mother, and you. "Do I smell lemon, Ma?" he would sing out in his most innocent tone. "I could swear I smell lemon." "Oh, hush up, Pa," Grandma would say, all flustered, "and leave the child alone." Grandpa would look quite innocent and say he just thought he smelled lemon—"didn't mean nothing by it." Your mother would come flying in telling you not to ruin your supper, Grandma would try to wriggle out of it, and you'd demolish the lemon drop. All the while Grandpa would sit over by the kitchen table trying to look serious and loving every minute of the ruckus. When the two women reached the height of their debate over the seriousness of a lemon drop, Grandpa would give you a conspiratorial wink as if to say: "Aren't these two making a silly fuss?"

There are no animated voices in the house now. You can hear only whispers coming from the other rooms. Your mother puts her arm around you; it's soft and a little damp from the heat. "You can see him now," she says. "But you must be very quiet and he won't be able to talk to you."

If you have any trouble returning to the present, fasten your attention on specific details in your immediate environment. Count the number of things in the room that are blue. Compare some shapes and sizes of objects. Focus on the sounds around you. Touch your chair, exploring the textures.

Notice that if you experienced strong emotions in this exercise they were evoked by the specific details of the memories, never because of an instruction you gave yourself to feel anything. Note that all the details in the *remember when* focus on people's actions and on images of things you touch, smell, taste, hear, and see. Don't attempt to conjure up feelings. The emotions will come. When you create your own *remember when*'s, keep the guidelines in mind.

This exercise functions as the "meat-and-potatoes" work when you are preparing for a role. In-character daydreaming and remembering your character's imaginary history will allow you to live in your character's skin until you are comfortable there. Then, when you are genuinely comfortable thinking as the character on-stage or in front of the camera, you will be able to trust yourself to respond without self-editing.

If I Were A Rich Man

Do your routine daily chores:

- *as if* you were waiting for a phone call telling you whether or not you got the lead in the play.
- *as if* you were a scientist about to attend a conference on dealing with nuclear waste.
- *as if* you were about to be married—in a few hours—to the woman, or man, of your dreams.
- *as if* you had just returned from burying a loved one.

The job should be at the center of your concentration. If you are painting a chair, simply paint the chair. Don't demonstrate that you are a scientist, or that you are going to be married. Paint the chair while allowing yourself to work in this imaginary framework you have invented. One advantage of this exercise is that you don't have to set aside a special time for the acting work. Combine this exercise with "Doing My Job" in Chapter 1. Pay careful attention to your driving, of course, while driving *as if* you were on your way to your wedding, an interview with a major Broadway producer, a funeral, or a vacation in Paris.

WHAT IF

Immerse yourself in an imaginary scenario stimulated by a "what if" question such as:

- What if I get a job on a soap this fall?
- What if I found out that my parents adopted me?
- What if that strange man across the mall approaches me and begins to talk to me?

MUSIC HATH CHARMS

Music is a powerful stimulant to the imagination. Play a favorite recording. Settle down in a comfortable chair, or lie on the floor allowing the music to carry you away to unfamiliar places and introduce you to unfamiliar people. Focus on the specifics of the pictures in your mind. Don't judge these journeys and don't insist on logic. If people with green hair pop into your imaginary sphere, enjoy them. Try this game with different styles of music. Instrumental forms are my favorites, since they provide my imagination maximum freedom. While lyrics may, in some cases, serve to stimulate my imagination, they also tend to pull me into someone else's story.

Many professional actors use music to help them make that leap into the character's domain. Experiment with this method of character exploration. Choose music your character would listen to—it may not suit your own tastes at all. Lose yourself in the tempos and rhythms. As you allow the music to influence your body and mind, you will gain invaluable insight into your character.

THE FAMILY ALBUM

Pick up an old photo album at an estate sale, find a book with portrait studies, or explore a history book that includes photos. Fabricate biographies for these people you don't know. Lose yourself in the particulars of facial features, clothing, objects, furniture, and architecture, then allow those elements to stimulate your imagination. Be specific. Imagine, in particular, the moment before the photo was shot. Let your mind wander freely through this unfamiliar world.

If you have the luxury of preparation time, this exercise can help you fill in the details of your character's history. Identify the people in the album who *know* your character, then create imaginary scenes weaving the people in the photos into your character's life. Allow all the elements of the photo including the faces, body language, and clothing to activate images in your unconscious.

GO INSIDE THE PICTURE

Choose a painting depicting a landscape, room, or courtyard. Use your imagination to enter the artist's setting and live there for a while. You might *visit* as yourself, or perhaps one of the characters in the picture will suggest to you someone you could be in that setting.

This exercise is useful for adding specifics to your character's given circumstances. For example, *go inside* the painting of a place where your character might have experienced significant events and conjure up action. Surrender to the intuitive discoveries triggered by the details in the painting. You will return from the visit armed with *memories* of events. Those events will provide your character with a more detailed and unique history and, in turn, a richer inner life.

CREATE YOUR OWN

I have described some of my favorite games. Don't limit yourself to these suggestions; devise new ones. For example, you could create imaginary histories for objects such as a silver tea service or a carved wooden box. Invent stories about two people you see standing at a bus stop or the person behind you at the check-out stand. Experiment with child-like flights of fancy.

You are already discovering that you can't deal with concentration and imagination separately. If you aren't able to hold the target of your choice at the center of your awareness, and if you haven't learned to silence your inner critic, the imagination games are tough sledding. Similarly, if you aren't able to imagine details that make your pretend reality more fascinating than your actual reality, you will have trouble getting your mind to pay attention. If this sounds like a Catch-22, don't despair. With patience and practice you can master both these skills.

Imagination is the very soul of the actor. Daydreaming, fantasizing, castle building, fabricating are all part of your essential homework. ENJOY!

FOOTNOTES

[1]Nazimova, p. 591.
[2]Irving Wallace, *Just Open A Vein*, edited by William Brohaugh (Cincinnati, Ohio: Writers Digest Books, 1987) p. 73.

Nature has given to men one tongue, but two ears,
that we may hear from others twice as much as we speak.
Epictetus, *Fragments*, No.113

CHAPTER 3

LEARNING TO LISTEN

Listen With Your Heart

Most actors have heard the old maxim "acting is simply listening." Unfortunately, some people don't understand that when one subscribes to that definition, it involves more than merely hearing one's cues. Actors may *hear* their cues, yet still get post-performance notes urging them to *listen*. The actor who listens heeds Stanislavski's counsel:

> If actors really mean to hold the attention of a large audience they must make every effort to maintain an uninterrupted exchange of feelings, thoughts, and actions among themselves.[1]

Underline "uninterrupted exchange." If you are to reflect human behavior, you must truly send and receive messages. You must *respond* to what happens around you or you will appear wooden and lifeless. Another pat definition for the craft that actors hear is, "Acting is reacting." There is merit in that simple statement.

Over the years I have grown accustomed to the protests some actors offer when they are cautioned to listen. Their defense is: "People don't always listen attentively 'in real life.'" That is certainly true. But, make no mistake about it, writers write about crucial moments in people's lives. In those circumstances, people don't often behave as they would in the "please-pass-the-potatoes" situations that abound in real life. Alfred Hitchcock summed it up when he said, "Drama is life with the dull bits cut out."[2]

EVERYDAY LISTENING

AN ACTIVE PROCESS

Since you want your listening on-stage to reflect human behavior, let's first look at the listening you do every day. To *hear* is to perceive sound by the ear. *Listening*, however, is a complex mental process involving not only hearing but several other faculties. I recall seeing a study, once, concluding that only 7% of communication is achieved by words—the rest is accomplished through facial expression, tone of voice, inflectional pattern, and body language. Clearly, you must use all your senses to listen effectively because if you only hear the words spoken you will be missing out on 93% of the potential communication. You will *hear* only 7% of what is being said to you. Think of how many times you've made statements like, "I don't like your tone," or "You look puzzled." Remarks like these clearly indicate that more than words play a role in communication. Some recent research suggests that when we actively listen, we not only hear what others are trying to communicate to us, we are even subject to what is called "mood contagion." We pick up all the messages—facial expression, body language, tone of voice, and inflectional pattern—from the sender; then we unconsciously mimic those signals and *catch* the other person's mood.

Listening involves not only hearing the sounds, or even words, but weighing the meanings and implications behind them. It also includes registering the message inherent in the speaker's tone of voice, inflectional pattern, facial expressions and body language. When you are listening, you not only hear sound, you process all the signals you are given—synthesizing those clues to deduce information. You assess the consequences of what is being said, test the truth of the statements, and search for motivations of the speaker. You consider solutions to a problem thrust upon you, defend yourself against accusations, prepare explanations for questions being asked, or delight in discoveries of common interest.

I SEE WHAT YOU MEAN

When you actively listen, you *see, hear, feel, smell* and *taste* what the speaker says. In other words, you generate visual images, have kinesthetic experiences, carry on internal dialogue or hear sounds, and experience olfactory (smell) or gustatory (taste) sensations. For most people, one of the systems tends to be reflected in the words, especially verbs, they most frequently use to communicate. Think about the common phrases we use to signal understanding: "I *see* what you mean," "I *hear* what you're saying" and "I *feel* exactly the same way." Three people describing the same experience might report: "I don't think you *see* my point of view," "I don't think you *hear* what I'm saying" or "I don't think you *feel* my *pain* here."[3]

Let me tell you about an experience an actor had in one of my classes recently. Jean had been struggling for several classes, then one day, after trying a new exercise, she suddenly began pumping her fists in the air and jumping around the room. She laughed and squealed, "I got it! I got it! I finally got it!" If you involved yourself in my story, you *sensed* the events. You probably *watched*, in your mind, a mini-motion picture of the event

I described. As you read the words, mental pictures of the story may have flashed across the "screen" in your mind and perhaps you *heard* the sounds. You may have *felt* sensations in your body similar to those I described. If you *heard* the story but failed to *listen*, the pictures, sounds and feelings were missing.

Our daily conversations overflow with stories like the one above—one or two sentence anecdotes, or long involved tales. Our stories serve varying functions. We use them to: entertain our listeners, illustrate points, justify our feelings or behavior, evoke empathy or sympathy, or share a significant experience. If the story is to fulfill its purpose, the storyteller and the listeners must share a complex series of internal representations.

Imagine that you have a story to tell and I am your listener. You begin by constructing vivid and specific mental representations of the events you want to relate. These representations cause you to consciously, and unconsciously, scan your memory for words that will convey those sensations. You will use facial expression, tone of voice, body language, and inflectional patterns to help transmit your experience to me. The communication succeeds only if I am expending a similar amount of mental energy. I must be willing to translate your words, facial expressions, tone of voice, body language, and inflectional patterns back into mental representations of sensory experiences. For your communication to be effective, my internal representations must resemble yours. Successful communication requires considerable mental activity on the parts of both speaker and listener. When that mental activity is absent, no listening occurs.

Listen To The Listener

In this imaginary conversation you and I are having, you not only listen when I speak, you listen while you are talking. While you are trying to get your message across by sending out all those verbal and physical signals to assist you in communication, you also take in messages from your listener. True listening isn't a "my turn, your turn" process. The sending out and the taking in of messages occur simultaneously. As I listen, I will send, in continuous waves, signals about agreement or disagreement, belief or disbelief, interest or boredom, understanding or misunderstanding, pleasure or annoyance. The sender is also receiving and the receiver is also sending. Only if you are listening to your listener, can you maintain an uninterrupted interchange of feelings, thoughts and actions.

Why You Don't Always Listen Well

In all likelihood, your everyday listening skills vary from excellent on one occasion to miserable the next. Becoming a better actor demands that you develop consistency in this area. It's easy to see the cause for some of the variations in your listening skills. You may hear everything a friend says about an attractive member of the opposite sex, then hear virtually nothing said by a complaining co-worker. You may hear the words of a song, then miss most of what a lecturer says, even though the lecturer's subject is important to you. You may hear every nuance of the conversation when eavesdropping on two people complimenting you, yet miss the details of your after-rehearsal critique.

You may not listen attentively for many reasons. For example, you may not be interested in the subject matter, or you may lack the physical energy. You may be distracted by a pressing problem, or maybe the speaker's message is complex and you give up in frustration. With sufficient motivation, organization, persistent effort, and—most important of all—improved concentration, you can overcome unsound listening habits. To be a better listener, however, you must also confront the fears and doubts that undermine listening.

- The fear that others won't approve of you
  If you believe that you are woefully inadequate and an unlovable person, you will carefully manage your behavior so that people don't see the *real* you. In that state, your inner critic is in charge, frantically trying to keep up appearances. That sort of self-monitoring doesn't leave any energy for taking in what's happening outside of you.

- Doubts about your ability to safely experience your emotions
  If you live in fear that you are on the verge of losing control, you will attempt to shut off your emotions. The best way to accomplish that is to filter out any information that could trigger an emotional response. If, in real life, you habitually shut out information you find disturbing, you're almost certain to do the same thing on-stage. Clearly, if you are preoccupied with self-defense—protecting yourself from anger, pain, fear, love, shame, surprise, or confusion—you can't afford to be truly attentive. More importantly, because you refuse to acknowledge anything that may hurt, frighten, embarrass, startle, or confuse you, you appear lifeless. By eliminating reaction, you eliminate action. Nothing much will happen in your scenes until you drop your protective shield. (See Chapter 4 for more help in this area.)

We will return to the subject of fears when we get to listening on-stage.

The bottom line is until you master concentration, your mind will wander. **You will never be a good listener until you can choose a target of attention and hold it at the center of your awareness.** You know that concentration follows interest. You will rely on your imagination to create interest in the speaker and the speaker's message. Now you begin to understand why I believe concentration and imagination are the two skills that are the foundation for all your other skills.

LISTENING ON-STAGE

First, let's be clear that effective listening on-stage is simply "real people listening." In other words, you trust yourself to listen just as you would in a real-life situation of similar intensity. You don't manipulate yourself into some state of mind that precludes all distracting thoughts, and you don't stifle the natural desire to talk while other people are talking. What you must do is achieve a level of concentration assuring that the distracting thoughts are character-thoughts and, of course, you observe normal rules of conversational courtesy whenever they are appropriate. Allowing your character the right to a mind that may wander momentarily will make him or her more human. A character who never has the urge to interrupt the speaker wouldn't resemble any person I know. If you insist on sustaining authentic conversations on-stage, you will listen naturally.

NO MUGGING PLEASE

We all have seen actors who have misinterpreted "acting is reacting." They manipulate their faces and bodies into what they think are meaningful responses to other characters' words or actions to show that they are listening. The result is painfully obvious over-acting. Not all your reactions need be externalized and made conspicuous to either the other characters or the audience. At the same time, what the other characters say must touch you, causing you to respond with internal adjustments. Without those internal adaptations that result from hearing what is said and those realignments of energy that inevitably result, you are acting alone and there is no interchange.

Take It Personally

Active listening also means you relate what you hear to your personal experiences. Everything we hear passes through the filter system created by our past. If you make the same statement to two people, each will *hear* a different message because no two people have the same history. If you mention to two people that you are going home for Thanksgiving, one may smile—assuming anticipation and delight—while the other extends condolences for a spoiled vacation. Each person responds according to his or her own family relationships and previous experiences connected with that holiday.

What you hear should pass through your character's personal filter system. With a powerful imagination you can invoke stored images, or recombine old experiences to create new images and make the character's events more fascinating to you than your actual past. Your powers of concentration then will enable you to focus your attention away from your actor-thoughts to your character-thoughts.

Take what is said to you personally. The other characters are talking to *you*—not to *him* or *her*. Often, when a scene isn't working, I ask the actors what is going on. One actor may say: "Well, she (the other character) is telling him (meaning the character he is playing) how she feels about ...." Wait! She is talking to **you**. You must be present in that moment as a participant, not an observer.

Don't Be Artificially Polite

Some actors who believe they have learned to listen well are only artificially polite. They stare at the speaking character, not daring to look away. They listen attentively, hanging on every word spoken by the other character, and wait breathlessly during long pauses. People don't usually listen to one another with that type of reverence. Observe people conversing. Even when the exchange is spirited, with all parties truly interested in what is being said, people are frequently distracted.

Think about the most recent conversation you had—choose one that included some dramatic tension to make this a fair comparison. Although you listened attentively, you didn't hang on every word said. Instead, you thought about your additions or rebuttals to what the other people were saying. You weighed offers and formulated counter-offers to proposals. You burned to inject your observation, or ask your question. Your mind may have wandered completely off the topic for a second here and there. Perhaps a comment evoked a distant memory. Maybe you were distracted by a disturbing problem brought to mind by another comment. You may have taken a little *break* to nurse a wound produced by a remark.

Not only did your mind dart about, your eyes moved as well. While some eye contact is a vital element of a genuine exchange, people do not stare fixedly into each other's eyes throughout a conversation. It is imperative that you learn to sustain eye contact with another person when it is called for. But, please don't become one of those actors who substitutes staring at people for authentic listening.

For your acting to be truthful, you must give yourself permission to listen to the other characters as you would in real life. Your impulse to speak while others are speaking is perfectly natural. After all, whatever triggers the thought responsible for your dialogue does not necessarily occur just as the other character stops speaking.[4] The key word or phrase that sets the process in motion may come at the *beginning* of a long speech. Out of deference to the speaker, you may inhibit your impulse to interrupt—still the impulse exists. Rest assured that your desire to over-talk doesn't always mean you aren't listening. To a certain extent, over-talking is essential if you want to reflect life-like behavior. You can expect to be criticized for over-talking if there is no interchange at all between you and the other characters. On the other hand, you must not be overly cautious about stepping on other people's lines. If you do, your stilted delivery will clearly signal to the audience that they are witnessing, not a genuine exchange, but a sham.

You Can't Fake It

If you, as the character, require a response before you can take the next step, physically or mentally, you must demand communication from the other character. On-stage, never pretend another character is communicating with you unless that pretense is a vital part of your character's action. The audience isn't blind and deaf—they will notice the lack of communication. Cope with the exchange of thoughts, feelings, and actions and what that means to you, *or* the lack of exchange and what that means.

What matters is what you are thinking and you must be thinking character-thoughts. If you listen to your actor self-talk or to what you think the audience is saying, you will be out of the scene and when you leave the scene, you take the audience with you. An audience isn't fooled by an actor who simply puts on a listening face. If you aren't affected by what is said to you—if there is no interchange of thought, feeling, and action—the audience will know that you are attempting to con them. Can you imagine how insulted you would be if you went to a football game and the players *pretended* to move a ball up and down the field?

Anchoring The Words In Action

You make it easier to be an active listener by anchoring the words in action. When you are an active listener in everyday life, you place the speaker's remarks into the specific framework of your own experience. When you play a character you must provide him or her with specific experiences—past events—that form a framework that is as specific as your own. (You will find more detailed instruction on anchoring words in action in several of the chapters in Parts Two and Three. For now, I just want to introduce this basic notion.) Let's suppose the other character says: "By the way, Dave will be joining us." You respond: "It will be nice to see him again." You need to create a framework of action that makes "Dave" a real person.

- Is this the Dave who lived next door to your family when you were growing up? Did Dave tease and torment your cat? Perhaps Dave called you "four eyes" when you were a teenager.

- Or, is this the Dave who had part-time jobs from the time he was ten years old and looked after his frail, old aunt. Did Dave restore a dilapidated used car when he was a teenager and spend hours polishing it every weekend? Perhaps you recall vividly the care he took waxing it and his celebratory drive around the neighborhood. Suppose you defended him when your sister ridiculed his affection for the old convertible.

Each of these choices establishes a unique framework for "Dave." The result is that when you hear his name, your mind is flooded with internal representations of the events you associate with him. Now your own line will resonate with authenticity. Provide those types of details for each of the moments in the script and you need never again work at *trying* to listen to your cue line.

When you have very little preparation time, you must exploit events in your memory bank for the details of your character's life. Some of those memories will come from your personal experiences, actual or vicarious. To recall those memories you will take advantage of reproductive imagination. Then, the further your character's experiences are from your own, the greater percentage of creative imagination you will use in your preparation. The more time you have to explore the material, the more particulars you provide. These details *load* the words with meaning. You can use this approach to make the character's situation vividly real. You make all the characters concrete by affording them a past littered with action.

Your character's concerns become valid because they exist in a specific framework of events. Consequently, you will have a reason to listen because you will have something at stake. You will listen because you have established expectations that will be either met or left unfulfilled. As a result, you will observe more carefully the other character. Every shrug, sigh, or clipped tone of voice takes on meaning. You will do more than perceive sound. You will pay attention. The words, along with the facial expressions, tone of voice, inflectional pattern, and body language, will resonate with meaning.

Have The Courage To Forget Your Lines

You may not listen on-stage because you worry about forgetting your lines. You may be afraid that if you commit to active listening, you will be distracted by the internal representations (visual images, inner dialogue and feelings) evoked by the speaker. Perhaps you fear that the distraction could cause you to "go up on your lines." Someone said (and I wish I knew who, so I could give proper credit): "Have the discipline to learn the lines and the courage to forget them." That is a key to listening on stage. You must invest the time it takes to assimilate the words. Then, in the moment of playing, you must have the courage to ignore the nagging of your inner voice as it coaches like a nervous prompter. You must be courageous enough to listen, instead, to the other characters and trust you will remember your lines precisely because of what the other people say to you.

(See Chapter 12 for more help with learning lines. You will also find that the chapter on triggers in *The Playing Is The Thing* will streamline the task of learning dialogue.)

In later chapters, ("Learning The Lines" and "Staying In Character," for example,) we will get to some skills that will help you be a better listener during performance. For now, let's focus on the basics of effective listening as they apply anywhere. As you develop your craft, you will continue to refine your listening skills.

Barring physical limitations, you have been listening all your life. Becoming an effective listener during performance may require nothing more than transferring that same skill to your work. On the other hand, if you listen haphazardly in your daily life, you will need to rid yourself of your bad habits. With practice you can learn to listen attentively.

EXERCISES

Keep these guidelines in mind when you hone your listening skills:

☛ **Anytime, Anywhere.**
Since you talk to people every day of your life, you won't have to set aside special time for homework; simply pay attention and make active listening a priority.

☛ **Baby Steps.**
The improvement in listening skills will come gradually. Don't expect miracles—you have invested years in perfecting your bad habits.

☛ **Create Desire.**
Listening is paying attention. You already know that you will pay attention only to what interests you. If you want to really *hear* what is being said to you, you must supply desire. Learn to generate interest in what the other person is saying; probe for all the hidden meanings; *see, hear* or *feel* what the other person is saying.

Everyday Stuff

Use everyday circumstances as opportunities for honing your listening skills. At least in the beginning, you are more likely to improve your skills during relatively low-key situations. Old habits are stubbornly ingrained. Don't expect the new you to suddenly emerge while explaining to your mother that you won't be home for Christmas, or conferring with a teacher who thinks your work isn't what it should be. While these are the very types of conditions in which skillful listening would be invaluable, the high pressure will likely cause you to revert to habitual behavior. Practice on the lady at the cleaners and the waiter where you eat lunch. You will find it is simpler to silence your inner critic when you have little at stake. Eventually you will use your improved listening skills even when your ego is on the line.

> ### Challenge

Choose a speaker on radio or television who is discussing a subject that doesn't interest you and create an interest in the subject. Find some thread by which you can connect to the thoughts being expressed. Even if you settle for proving what a jerk this character is, you have motivated yourself to pay attention.

> ### What Did You Say?

For this book I wanted to focus on exercises you can do alone. Nevertheless because this is one of my favorites, I am including this one even though it requires a partner.

Run a scene with another actor; it may be a cold reading or memorized work. Before you respond with your line, as written, repeat what was said to you, or say something that clearly shows you heard what was said. This exercise is much easier to demonstrate in a class than it is to explain in a book, even so I think, if you experiment with the following example, you will discover the usefulness of this approach.

The dialogue will go something like the example below. (The writer's words for the character are in **bold** type; the actor's words are in *italics*.)

She

What do you want?

He

What do I want?
Oh, you think you have the world by the tail, don't you?

She
(over-talking)

I think I have the world by the tail?

He
(continuing)

Let me tell you a thing or two, hot shot.

She

Oh, yeah, let me tell you a thing or two.
Get out of my office!

He

Lady, I'm not about to get out of your office.
I have very expensive tastes. My wife has expensive tastes.

She
(over-talking)

I don't care about your expensive tastes.

He
(continuing)
And that account means a lot to me.

She
(over-talking)
It means a lot to me, too. Now
**Are you going to leave? Or do I have to call
someone?**

I caution you: Don't turn this exercise into an excuse for not learning your lines or for rewriting the author's dialogue. Too many actors find ad-libbing irresistible and discover dozens of excuses for not learning the script as written. This is strictly an exercise; don't take it on-stage, or in front of the camera. Unless you are certain that you have permission to improvise dialogue, don't. In performance, when you have the impulse to say the words in italics, channel that impulse into the writer's words.

Follow A Good Example

Study a videotape of a well-made film. Note that character A's impulse to speak most often occurs *during* character B's line rather than after B has finished speaking. The listener is not impassively hearing what the other characters are saying. He or she is silently responding to the speaker, either resisting or acquiescing. Notice the over-talking. Observe the interchange of feelings, thoughts and actions.

If you acknowledge whether what you are saying, or not saying, is helping you convey your message, you will be motivated to listen. You will listen for the clues that tell you whether you are succeeding or failing and you will be truly talking to someone, not just perceiving sound and saying words. In real life, you use words to help you exchange information with other people. Simultaneously, you are influenced by others trying to *get through* to you. Only this kind of truthful behavior will create life on stage or in front of the camera. **Acting is "simply listening" provided you realize we are talking about *active* listening and active listening means affecting the other characters and being affected by them.** Learn to listen with your heart and mind as well as your ears.

FOOTNOTES

[1]Constantin Stanislavski, *An Actor Prepares,* p. 186.

[2]Alfred Hitchcock. Quoted by Leslie Halliwell in *Halliwell's Filmgoer's and Videoviewers's Companion, 10th edition*, edited by John Walker (New York: Harper Collins Publishers, Inc., 1993) p. 379.

[3]Richard Bandler and John Grinder present a fascinating look at mental representation in *Frogs Into Princes* (Moab, Utah: Real People Press, 1979).

[4]For a more detailed discussion of triggers see my book on games and exercises, *The Playing Is The Thing* (Burbank, CA: Wolf Creek Press, 1996).

There is a great deal of unmapped country within us.

George Eliot, *Daniel Deronda*

Though we disguise our feelings pretty well,
What we mean by 'very good' is 'Go to hell.'
Noel Coward, *Bitter Sweet*, Act I, sc.ii

CHAPTER 4

RECLAIMING YOUR EMOTIONS

I Yam What I Yam

When you concentrate despite distractions, enjoy a vivid and rich imagination, and listen with your head *and* your heart, you possess the skills that form the rudimentary foundation for your craft. It is even possible that you will work professionally before you develop skills much beyond these fundamentals. Because of a highly commercial *look* or *quality*, personal connections, good luck, perseverance, or all the above, you may get cast—you may even become successful. If, on the other hand, you hope to be an exceptional actor, plan to bring your emotions to your work. The emotions add the texture, or the spice, to the performance. You can produce acceptable work armed with only the rudiments, but you won't deliver outstanding work until you gain access to your emotions.

EARLY TRAINING

Most psychologists agree that the list of human emotions is a short one. Seldom is the catalogue longer than: *mad, glad, sad, afraid, loving, hurt, surprised, ashamed, disgusted*. As an infant, you were born with the innate ability to experience and express the full range of these emotions. Your experiences in childhood and in life, to date, have shaped your current emotional range.

Your parents knew that throwing food would not get you invited to many dinner parties. They understood that refusing to share your toys would not help you win friends, and hitting everyone who made you angry would get you in a heap of trouble. So, the grown-ups in your world set out to socialize you. Socialization included teaching you that certain *behaviors* are deemed unacceptable by our society. Chances are, however, the adults around you failed to make the distinction between your behavior and your feelings. If this was true in your case, you learned not only to inhibit certain behaviors, you learned that the people bigger than you were easier to get along with when you inhibited many of your emotions. They left you believing that your natural emotional responses were "bad," "stupid," or, at least, inappropriate. For example, you may have learned that it was not wise to *hear* things that made you angry because your anger got you in trouble with the adults who were in charge. Perhaps someone even punished you because of your feelings. Maybe you learned to avoid criticism or punishment by shutting out messages that hurt you or frightened you because your pain was ridiculed, or dismissed by the grown-ups who made the rules.

Being adaptable, you quickly learned which emotional responses the adults in your household were looking for, then you learned how to manufacture those reactions. In some cases, the grown-ups probably gave you specific instructions regarding emotions. For example, if you behaved badly because you were angry, someone may have condemned your emotion rather than your actions. ("Nice little girls don't get angry.") Perhaps your feelings were denied ("You're not angry; I know you better than that.") You may have been encouraged to substitute an acceptable feeling or sensation for one that was not tolerable. ("You're not angry; you're just tired.")

You also learned the degree to which it was safe to experience and express your emotions through modeling the people who raised you. For example, if you had parents who never expressed anger, you probably learned from them to suppress your anger. You also may have learned to blunt your feelings by denying your wants or needs. Provided that you don't admit, even to yourself, that you want to accomplish something, failure doesn't produce disappointment nor does success evoke celebration. For example, when you were a child, you clearly knew when you needed someone to hold and comfort you. But, you may have discovered that not only would your needs be unmet, they made your parents uneasy. If so, you learned to repress your wants, having discovered that denial was less stressful than rejection.

Through these types of experiences, you may have become an expert at denying your emotional response to the actions of the people around you. It's possible that you have buried your feelings so long you confused even yourself. If you substitute acceptable feelings for authentic ones long enough, eventually, you don't notice that you are making the adjustments.

REMOVE THE MASK

You may have bought into the illusion that you *are* the poses and attitudes you use to control your emotions. For example, perhaps you smile when people say hurtful things to you, telling yourself that it really doesn't bother you. The truth is you have been denying the pain and putting up the front so long the lie is habitual. You are no longer aware of the effort it takes to repress the pain and put on that smile. If you have bought into the poses and attitudes, it is likely that you most often portray stereotypical characters. It is no wonder. You may see yourself only as a stereotype. You may think of yourself as a two-dimensional figure: "the good little girl," "the tough guy", "the sensitive young man," "the nurturing earth mother." The more desperately you need to sustain the role you have created for yourself, the harder it is for you to imagine a character who is something other than a type. If you have been playing "the good little girl" or "the tough guy" role faithfully for years, you honestly believe that this is typical human behavior—everyone playing a role. You must acknowledge that the pose you have assumed is part of an act, a cover-up for feelings. Underneath that pose is a human being—an emotional being—capable of contradictions and surprises.

Before you rush to defend your cover-ups, remember they are *man-made*. They are synthetic and limited. Compare the pose to a mask you might use to cover your face. Regardless of how carefully constructed the mask may be, it will never produce all the subtlety and nuance of a human face. Despite artful design, the mask will never have the mobility, the life, and the light of a human face. It may fascinate me in the beginning, but I will rapidly lose interest in the unchanging expression. Your cover-ups, your attitudes and poses, act as a mask obscuring the contradictions and nuances that make you unique. While the mask may interest me for a few moments, soon I will grow tired of its single expression and long for the surprises of what lies hidden beneath it. Chip away at the cover-ups by reclaiming your emotions. It may take you years to uncover the authentic self hidden beneath the disguise, even so each tear you make in that mask will pay off in your acting.

Take advantage of every possible avenue to reestablish communication with your inner being. Professional counseling, academic courses in psychology, and self-directed reading courses can help you reclaim your emotions. Although professional guidance will probably accelerate your progress, you can initiate the self-examination on your own. Let's begin with some observations on the nature of emotions, how you can reclaim access to yours, and how they relate to your acting. In Chapter 15, "Feelings," we will return to this subject and explore the role emotions play in your work.

EMOTIONS ARE EFFECTS AND ACTIONS ARE THE CAUSE

Many people, and not just actors, mistakenly believe that emotions are simply things that happen to them. Feelings do not come over us from out of the blue. You aren't just walking along a sidewalk and some *sad* falls off a ledge and hits you. Emotions are effects. The causes of emotions are:

1. Events, either real or imagined.
2. Our perception of those events, or what we think about them.

If you are sad, you suffered a loss. The loss may have occurred moments ago or years ago. Perhaps it was a loss of property, affection, opportunity, or face—still the loss is the cause and the emotion is the effect. Once you are clear about this cause and effect relationship, you minimize the temptation to reduce every acting consideration to a matter of emotion. Real people simply do not go about randomly experiencing emotions. In your exercises to help you reconnect with your feelings, you will have to supply actions and events as *causes*, remembering that the emotions are *effects*.

What The Child Needs

When you were a child—before the repression and manipulation set in—you not only experienced your emotions and needs, you expressed them freely, both orally and physically. When you were hungry, you cried. If you wanted something, you grabbed it and, if someone took it away from you, you were furious and you screamed. You may have reached for the object, trying to grab it back. As you grew older you put words to your action: "Mine!" When Mommy and Daddy said good-bye, you cried and screamed, "No"—all the while reaching out to your parents as if you could stop them. If something struck you as funny, you laughed noisily and maybe you pointed at what amused you; it didn't matter to you if you were in church and everyone else was having a solemn moment. If something frightened you, you screamed in terror and clung desperately to your mother's skirt, holding on for dear life.

The things that make you angry now are quite different—you have learned to share, you laugh at different things, and other things frighten you. Nevertheless, you still experience, down deep, the same intense emotions you experienced as a child. The difference is that, because you are socialized, you have modified your behavior and you probably don't experience your feelings as freely. For example, rather than experiencing simple, unadulterated fear, you may cover the fear with hostility or deny that the fear exists. If someone hurt you when you were very young, you said, "Ouch! Don't do that." Now you may smile and convince yourself that the person who hurt you "really didn't mean anything by that comment." The smile and the rationalization are cover-ups—they distort your perception of the action that has occurred. When you smile, pretending nothing has hurt you, you deny the actions of the other person. While you may believe that this coping mechanism works in real life, it is toxic to your acting. If you consistently deny the actions of the other characters in your scene, that is a certain way to make the playing dull. By continually telling me through your behavior that nothing is happening, you convince me that there is no reason for me to pay attention. I will believe you and I will rapidly lose interest.

Connect with your basic childlike needs and emotions even though their intensity may seem inappropriate to the scene. **Even when it may not be appropriate to express the demands, these deeply felt *uncivilized* desires are motivating you.** Nowadays, you don't shout, "Ouch, you hurt me," or "Give it back. It's mine," and you don't clutch your mother's skirt while you scream in terror. However, the reason you don't say and do those things is the early socialization—it doesn't mean the needs and the feelings no longer exist. Enrich your work by rediscovering your authentic needs and emotions and don't worry about this causing you to come across as an irrational being. Find the courage to awaken the emotional primitive that lives in all of us.

Emotions Are In Your Body

Emotions aren't intellectual concepts; they are visceral experiences. It is no coincidence that we commonly describe our emotions using the word *feelings* while we use the same word to describe the function of perceiving by touch. Even in our language we acknowledge that emotions are physical sensations. Emotions aren't things that reside exclusively in your head. They exist in your body—specifically in the *viscera*: the soft interior organs in the body cavities (especially those in the trunk) such as heart, lungs, stomach, liver and intestines. Often, when we describe our feelings to one another, we unconsciously acknowledge the true nature of our emotions. We say things such as: "I have this knot in my stomach." "My heart is breaking." "Get off my back." "The guy's a pain in the neck." "My heart was in my throat."

Move your feelings out of your head and into your body by conceding that what you frequently refer to as emotions are actually no more than intellectual assessments. If you don't experience any physical responses, while describing what you are feeling, you are fooling yourself. Anytime you identify your emotions, you should be using that short list: mad, glad, sad, afraid, loving, hurt, surprised, ashamed, disgusted. Otherwise, you are probably referring to attitudes, or poses, that you have adopted to cover your feelings. For example, actors constantly tell me that their sarcasm was "how I felt at the moment." No one *feels* sarcastic. Sarcasm is a cover-up for pain or anger you choose not to express. To clarify the differences between emotions and attitudes, pay attention to your body and notice that genuine emotional responses affect you physically.

This Isn't An Excuse To Get Crazy

Do <u>not</u> misinterpret any of this material as an instruction to *express* all your feelings. If you make that mistake you will probably lose a lot of friends and almost certainly lose any jobs you get. Part of what we all do to make society work is to recognize and inhibit anti-social behavior. If every time I'm angry, I blow up and scream at everyone or hit people, I'll probably be left alone, fired and maybe even locked up. Even so, this must not preclude my *feeling* angry; it should only inhibit anti-social *behavior*. In addition, please don't construe any of this advice as an endorsement for *nursing* emotions such as anger, guilt, fear or pain. To experience an emotion is very different from holding onto feelings. You shouldn't ever have to deny the existence of your emotions, although you may frequently find it advisable to behave in a way that does not reflect your feelings. This advice applies to both your everyday life and your acting.

Start The Reclamation Process Now

Before you can bring the full range of your emotions to your work, you need to re-establish the connection to the part of your consciousness that involves feelings. Give yourself permission, if you haven't already, to reclaim the full range of your passions. Although you do not have to express your emotions, you must be able to experience the people and events around you with feelings of anger, sadness, joy, fear, disgust, surprise, shame, and love. Part of your job is to reveal the emotional life of your character; however, if you aren't able to access your own emotions you can't expect to accomplish that. The only feelings you have to work with are your own. You don't need to acquire some feelings—you were born with the capacity for the full range of emotions. Moreover, everyone else has exactly the same range. Your challenge is to reclaim access to the emotions you may have learned to deny. When acting is listless and flat, it is usually because the actors have shut off their awareness of emotions, thus rendering themselves lifeless. Life and feelings are inseparable; feelings are energy.

Becoming an exceptional actor is partly about breaking down inhibitions, and this is a frightening process because the giving up of boundaries set by the ego-self feels like a loss of self. For example, if you learned to smile when you were hurt—and that has *worked* for you up to this point—it's pretty scary to give up the smile. When you do, you expose your pain and risk the ridicule or hostility your feelings may evoke. If you give up your defense mechanisms, someone may hurt you, shame you, terrify you, or send you into an uncontrollable rage—and all this under public scrutiny. You risk uncertainty if you are swept away by pure joy or genuine love. This is a gamble worth taking because giving up the self-restraint that protects you from emotions is, in reality, a reclamation of your complete self. You aren't your defense mechanisms—they are mere appendages, protective devices that you grafted onto the real you because you craved emotional security.

Unfortunately, there is no foolproof technique for reclaiming your emotions and no magic pill to swallow that makes it easier. You can, however, begin to break down your inhibitions provided you have: an honest desire to be more vulnerable, the courage to endure the failures, and the discipline to keep working at it.

EXERCISES

Keep these guidelines in mind as you practice the exercises:

☞ **Most important of all, remember: emotions are effects.**
Supply the causes, or events, and the emotions will follow.

☞ **Don't expect miracles.**
Of all the exercises you do, these are the ones most likely to produce frustration. Your progress will probably be slow. You are attempting to rid yourself of inhibitions you spent years perfecting. Be patient and keep working.

☞ **The goal is experience, not just understanding.**
Don't get sidetracked by trying to understand your emotions; your goal is to experience your feelings. Don't turn this into an intellectual exercise. If you aren't experiencing the emotions in your body, you are hiding in intellectual descriptions of feelings and you should be clear about the difference between the two.

☞ **You can't *will* yourself to experience an emotion.**
You must be receptive to feelings, yet resist the temptation to direct your experience of these exercises. Whatever you feel is what you feel. Don't edit your emotions.

☞ **Ask for help if you need it.**
Don't attempt to deal with deeply painful, unresolved issues without some emotional support. The purpose of this work is to help you reconnect with your emotions. On the other hand, the procedures here are not adequately designed to help

you work out serious personal issues that may require the help of a professional counselor. Even though you are cautious, some of this work may reopen painful emotional wounds. You may want to ask a friend to be with you, in case you have trouble returning to the present. You might at least contact a friend before you begin the work, requesting that the person check in on you at a set time. (Review the instructions for the *remember when* in Chapter 2.)

☞ **We'll be back.**

These are some basic exercises for your personal development. We will continue the work on emotions in Parts Two and Three—"Exploring The Script" and "Allowing The Part To Play You."

KEEPING COUNT

This is the workhorse exercise for developing awareness of your emotions. Do the exercise faithfully and don't judge your progress.

Keep a daily count of the times you repress or cut off your feelings. For example, you may pretend to be "just fine" to make everyone else comfortable, when in reality you are furious or deeply hurt.

The point of this exercise is not to "fix what is wrong with you," but to enhance your awareness of your emotions and to improve your ability to experience them. Record the instances of repression throughout the day. (Make a ball-point pen mark on your wrist, move objects from one pocket to another, or make a paper clip chain; be creative in your scorekeeping system.) You may not realize you have denied your emotions until several hours (even days, weeks—or years in worst case scenarios) have passed. Set aside a reflection period (at the beginning or end of the day) to review the number of times during the preceding day you pretended to feel something you weren't feeling.

Without judging or criticizing yourself for the denial of your emotions, acknowledge your feelings and validate them. Remind yourself, as though you were a small child being taught, that it was okay to feel what you were feeling. Congratulate yourself for recognizing your emotions. Gradually, you will notice that the moment of recognition is less and less removed from the event. The ideal would be to reach a point where you have blanket permission to feel whatever you are feeling twenty-four hours a day despite other people's needs. However, don't get crazy over reaching that ideal; aim, instead, toward a greater awareness. (I remind you that this does not mean you should *express* all of your feelings.)

REMEMBER WHEN

Use the *remember when* exercise in Chapter 2, "Developing Your Imagination." Create an emotionally charged situation that did happen, or could have happened, to you as a small child and experience the event through the magic of imagination. Stay focused on the physical actions (what people did) and detailed descriptions of your surroundings (What was the temperature? What were you wearing? Could you hear any music?) Instead of trying to recreate feelings, allow the emotions to emerge out of the action. Here are some examples to get you started:

- Enter the living room of the house you lived in as a child and show your mom and dad how you hurt your finger. Ask for the comfort you need.

- Imagine that your mother and father are going out for the evening—they will leave you with the baby sitter. Persuade your parents not to go away and leave you.
- Your brother or sister has taken your favorite toy. Demand its return.

GET YOUR BODY INTO IT

Place two chairs facing one another, as if for conversation. Sit in one chair and imagine one of your parents sitting in the other. Explore these basic needs by telling your mother or father what you need. ("Hold me—I'm scared." "Give it back—it's mine." "Don't leave me." "Go away.") Use your hands and arms to help you communicate your needs to the imagined parent. Your goal is to get the emotions evoked out of your head and into your body. Resist all those urges to be rational. This is about how you feel, not how you ought to behave.

Reclaiming your capacity to experience and express your feelings may seem an overwhelming task. This is the part of the restoration process I mentioned in "Freeing The Actor Within" that will make you wish you could start from the ground up rather than having to rehabilitate an existing entity. It is a long, arduous process, still you're going to be living in the confines of your consciousness the rest of your life. It's worth however much sweat it takes to renovate this *house*, and, regardless of how attached you may be to your cover-ups, you can turn this situation around. After all, you learned to inhibit your feelings. You can just as well train yourself to become aware of those inhibitions and resist the urge to deny your emotions. You cannot afford to skip this part of the training—without it you cannot expect to bring authenticity to your work. Besides, if you won't tackle this job for your craft, do it to enrich your life. Live your life authentically, making choices to manage your behavior without denying your emotions.

When I leave home to walk to school
Dad always says to me,
'Marco, keep your eyelids up
And see what you can see.'
And to Think that I Saw
It on Mulberry Street

CHAPTER 5

OBSERVATION

Hold the Mirror Up To Nature

If your acting is to resonate with authenticity, you must be certain that you have stored in your consciousness reliable models of human behavior. The abundance and accuracy of your mental storehouse will depend on your powers of observation. You should be constantly exercising those powers and accumulating raw material for true-to-nature character development and genuine interaction. Utilize all the sources available to you. An obvious mother lode is the work of your fellow artisans. Study their performances in movies, on stage, or on television. Your video cassette recorder is an invaluable study tool. Rent a film and watch it several times, giving yourself an opportunity to absorb, both consciously and intuitively, what the actors are doing. Notice how simple eloquent acting is, how economical it is.

While you will profit by learning from your fellow actors, you also should heed Hamlet's advice to the players and "hold, as 'twere, a mirror up to nature." Study human beings in action. Stake out a booth in a diner. Arm yourself with a book, a newspaper, or pad and pencil (so your intentions will not be obvious) then soak up some real life by listening and watching people behave. Find a place to *pitch your tent*—in a hotel lobby, at the airport, in a hospital waiting area (any place where people congregate and you can fade into the background), and study the people around you. Schedule your TV time to include some authentic reality-based programming. Watch people who aren't performers.

Notice how phony some acting looks in comparison with actual human behavior. Real listening is wonderfully simple and reacting often means *doing* nothing—engaging only in mental activity. (Occasionally what is billed as reality-based involves people putting on a show. You'll have to become a discriminating viewer.)

Observation of people in everyday circumstances allows you to mentally file specific examples of human expression during communication. You can note personal eccentricities of speech, vocal patterns, facial expressions, and body language. You will be soaking up samples of body use such as posture and gait while you store, in your consciousness, invaluable models of emotional life. You will have an opportunity to see the difference between the behavior of real people dealing with events and what is often passed off as human behavior by careless actors.

Don't get bogged down in analysis or organization of what you are observing. Much of the learning process occurs on an unconscious level. Concentrate on truly *seeing*. In other words, watch people with interest and curiosity. If you regularly observe people and if you spend time recreating your subjects, you will stockpile in your mind and body valuable material for future roles. By arming your unconscious mind with images modeled on real people, you produce a profound effect on your acting.

EXERCISES

Keep these guidelines in mind as you practice the exercises:

☛ **The urge to mimic is innate.**
Aristotle wrote,

> Poetry [drama] in general seems to have sprung from two causes, each of them lying deep in our nature. First, the instinct of imitation is implanted in man from childhood, one difference between him and other animals being that he is the most imitative of living creatures, and through imitation learns his earliest lessons; and no less universal is the pleasure felt in things imitated.[1]

Practice these exercises until you trust your instinct to imitate. Notice how naturally and joyfully small children mimic what they see.

☛ **Use your eyes and your heart, not just your head.**
Study the subject with your eyes and with your heart—don't simply analyze the person. This shouldn't be an intellectual exercise. The final goal is imitation, not a description.

☛ **Concentration is the key.**
These are exercises in concentration—your inner critic will plague you for attention. As is true in any test of concentration, you must find a way to make the target more fascinating than your distractions. The subject of observation is the giraffe here, and

your own personal concerns are the elephant. (See Chapter 1, "Training Your Mind To Focus On Your Mental Target.")

☛ **Fire the judge.**
Resist the temptation to judge or evaluate your subject. Allow yourself, instead, to merge with the subject.

☛ **Open yourself to sensory stimulation.**
Open yourself to unfamiliar sensory experiences—experiences that, in a sense, aren't your own. Commitment to this mimicry, will enable you to see through someone else's eyes, hear with different ears, and touch with unfamiliar tactile awareness.

☛ **Surrender.**
Through the magic of imagination, think with your subject's mind—feel with your subject's heart. Surrender to the needs of the person you are observing.

☛ **Start small.**
Make your first sessions brief to avoid overload. Repeat the first exercise until you are proficient, then advance to the next level.

☛ **Repetition is the secret.**
If you feel uneasy and awkward when you begin using your innate ability to mimic, frequent practice will eventually eliminate the discomfort.

Fade Into The Wallpaper

Hang out in a nearby coffee shop or diner. Arm yourself with a newspaper, or a book to help you *fade into the wallpaper*. Pick a customer and make that person the center of your awareness. Focus on the details of your subject's behavior—picking up the fork, chewing the food, using the napkin. Be aware of posture, body language, gestures, and facial expression. Allow yourself to experience, vicariously, your subject's actions with your own muscles. Notice that we do this naturally when we watch someone who is engaged in an activity that fascinates us. When the basketball player feints to the right to fake out an opponent, we *feel* the movement in our own muscles. Permit your body to take on the posture of the person you are observing.

When you get home, allow your body to remember the experience. Recreate the actions of the person you observed. The secret is to concentrate on the specific details of the person's actions. Don't try to *play the character*. Just repeat the simple actions—pick up the fork, chew the food, use the napkin—and allow your body to remember what you saw and felt.

Walk In The Moccasins

Return to the coffee shop and study a serving person or busboy this time. Give the same attention to detail—writing the order, putting the cup of coffee on the table, etc. Now you will add awareness of carriage and gait. You will be absorbing tempo and rhythm of the movement as the person moves about in a larger space.

When you recreate the subject at home, follow the instructions for "Fade Into The Wallpaper." Pay attention to details. Don't play the character.

THE EARS HAVE IT

You could pick a new person or return to the subject for "Walk In The Moccasins." This time pay attention to vocal patterns. Tune your ear to each eccentricity: dialect, rhythm, tempo, energy, and emphasis. Get the speech patterns into your body.

When you recreate your subject, remember to stay focused on simple details. Don't get sidetracked onto performance.

A DOUBLE SCOOP

Choose two people who are interacting and observe the over-talking that naturally occurs in conversation. Notice that the tempos and rhythms vary constantly. Note that people aren't displaying their emotions; instead, they are attempting to communicate successfully and emotions are a by-product. Allow your mind and body to absorb the intricate rhythms of everyday speech. Ultimately, careful observation of real conversation will encourage you to literally talk to the other characters in the scene rather than act as if you're talking to them.

GRADUATION

Put one of your characters in an improvised situation. For example, take your waiter or waitress out of the coffee shop. Imagine, in detail, this person's apartment or house and invent, for him or her, a sequence of logical actions. At that point, recreate the character with your body and carry out the actions as the character. Keep repeating the simple actions until you feel you have succeeded in performing each action *as* the character.

Expand on this basic exercise by doing your own chores while using your body as though it were the body of the person observed.

Practice these exercises until they become habitual. Imitation is an instinct of your nature. Indulge regularly in this child's play and you will accumulate a rich storehouse of material for your work.

FOOTNOTES
[1]*Aristotle's Poetics*, translated by S. H. Butcher (New York: Hill and Wang, 1968) p. 55. Copyright Francis Fergusson, 1961.

The mind is its own place, and in itself
Can make a heaven of hell, a hell of heaven.
John Milton, *Paradise Lost*, Bk. 1

CHAPTER 6

LEARNING TO RELAX

Take A Deep Breath

Every professional, from the Hawaiian scrimshaw artist creating a delicate blossom to the NBA player sinking a three-pointer, knows that an effective performance depends upon a suitable level of relaxation. You cannot use either your mind or body well unless you are appropriately relaxed. Even ordinary daily tasks require the proper balance of muscular tension and relaxation. Try cutting a piece of paper while you hold the scissors in a hand that is rigid and this simple everyday job becomes nearly unmanageable. If, in contrast, you let your hand go totally limp, the task is impossible. You can use the scissors effectively only if you balance the amount and degree of tension and relaxation.

Recall an occasion in your life when you were fully absorbed in an activity, and performing effectively. Think of any activity including acting, reading, participating in a sport, engaging in a stimulating conversation, listening to some favorite music, or experiencing erotic arousal. Now search your memory for one of those moments when you were performing at your peak and you were either rigid with physical and mental tension or so relaxed you were about to fall asleep. You couldn't think of any, could you? In every instance you were *appropriately* relaxed.

I frequently see dull work done by actors who don't understand the balance between tension and relaxation. They are impassive because they are either limp from total relaxation, or rigid with excess tension. The overly relaxed actor forgets that absolute relaxation is the state just before falling asleep—hardly the condition you want to be in when you perform. You produce exciting work when you are in a heightened state of awareness, especially sensitive to everything around you. On the other hand, the actor who is rigid with fear is unable to bring the character to life because there is no psychic or physical energy left over to devote to the character's concerns.

Being appropriately relaxed while acting means that you are free of all nervous tension related to you, the actor. You experience, then, only anxieties and tensions belonging to the character. There are many useful techniques in Parts II and III, ("Exploring The Script" and "Allowing The Part to Play You") that will help you achieve this balance. At the end of this chapter, you will find some relaxation exercises. But before we get to the exercises, let's look at nervous tension.

Self-Talk Can Turn Muscles Into Armor

If you suffer from *brain-lock* and your muscles are rigid with fear, whether on-stage or in real life, you may think that is "how you are." On the contrary, you probably created the apprehension with your self-talk—unless, of course, there actually is a saber-tooth tiger in the room, or this particular audience has resorted to shooting actors whose performances they disdain. In other words, you shifted your attention away from your character-objectives and filled your mind with scary stories about events you were experiencing or expected to experience. That type of inner dialogue will inevitably cause you to brace your body for fight or flight.

If, for example, you told yourself that you will never be able to cry in the second act, or you will make a fool of yourself trying to play a part for which you are too tall/thin/fat/young/old, you are bound to be upset. If you conjure up images of yourself failing, your entire body will respond to that dread of failure. Fear is a powerful emotion and the fear of failure, or loss of face, is a universal one. Your muscles tense, your heartbeat quickens, and your breathing becomes shallow. If you threaten yourself with images of disapproval from "important" people, you probably will become anxious. In response to the anxiety, you may turn your muscles and tendons into armor. If you habitually make yourself anxious and you normally cope by making your body a rigid protective device, you may have come to believe that this is your natural state. You may no longer realize you are putting the armor on and you may not know how to remove it. If so, you need to learn physical relaxation.

Relaxation techniques are invaluable to you in everyday life and critical to your craft. If your muscles have become armor, your body is a rigid container that suffocates your emotions. Emotions are composed of not only your thoughts but the physical responses of your body. Muscular tension erects an almost impregnable fortress around your solar plexus causing you to feel detached. In this impassive state, you could only reveal to us a character who is mostly numb to emotional stimuli. If you are consumed by doubts and fears, you can't possibly commit your mental and physical energies to the character's needs. Help your body form new habits by learning relaxation techniques. Be sure, however, to make this a two-pronged attack by improving your self-talk.

THERE ARE SOLUTIONS

THE KEY TO RELAXATION

Here is the secret to relaxation: **get your attention off yourself**. It's that simple. Suppose I ask you to show me how you walk. Unless you are a model, or uncommonly confident, you will probably become self-conscious. Perhaps you have a moment of panic, then begin moving and watching yourself. You may squirm under what you assume is scathing scrutiny, since you imagine I wouldn't have asked you to do this if I hadn't intended to judge your performance. With all your attention on your now uncooperative limbs, you try to walk *well* and begin to feel as though you were being asked to invent walking. You *try* to walk rather than just walk because you have no motivation for moving except to show yourself in a favorable light. Perhaps your mouth gets dry, your shoulders tense, your heartbeat quickens every so slightly, and your breathing becomes a little more shallow. You never dreamed walking could be so difficult.

Now assume, instead, that I ask you to get that book across the room for me and you generously oblige. You will stride effortlessly across the space. Perhaps you will be preoccupied by whatever thoughts you were already entertaining. Maybe you will wonder why I requested the book and didn't get it myself, or even wonder if I am playing some trick on you. But you will not be thinking about how to walk and you will not be consumed by the anxiety that attends self-judgment. When your attention is off yourself, you can function at peak efficiency.

Put yourself under the microscope of judgment and you can produce instant anxiety. Commit to a goal or intention and you fill your consciousness with the tasks you must complete to achieve that goal. At that point, there is no room in your mind, or body, for anxiety.

STARVE THE FEAR

When we talk about fear and cleaning up your self-talk, we are elaborating on the concept of putting your attention outside yourself. Let's look more specifically at the way you talk to yourself when you are fearful. Begin by replacing scary ideas with thoughts that are more productive. By changing your focus and replacing the inner dialogue, you can substitute purpose for anxieties. For example, rather than imagining failure while you prepare for an audition, celebrate your opportunity to perform. Lucky you. You get to do what you love doing. Get your mind off your doubts by thinking, instead, about a fellow actor's need for support. When rescuing someone else, you haven't time for your uneasiness. Focus on the poor auditors. That will get your mind off yourself. What a job they have. It is a daunting task, picking the right actors from a sea of hopefuls most of whom the auditors have never seen before. People who make casting decisions have fears too. If they select the wrong actors, the project fails and the person who made those casting choices looks bad. You see, you aren't the only one with problems.

Your ultimate goal is to eliminate any fears that paralyze you. Meanwhile, these diversions, or *mind tricks,* I have just described will reduce the death grip of apprehension. That frees you to do your job. Still, the best part about avoiding scary thoughts is yet to come. Eventually, you will reap a genuine windfall. Fear is a voracious beast. When you stop feeding it scary thoughts, it will wither from starvation. In the meantime, while you are learning to conquer your fears, stop wasting energy trying to hide the ones that persist. Struggling to cover your apprehension requires enormous energy and produces paralyzing physical and mental tension.

Surrender To The Character's Needs

The best way to get your attention off yourself is to hold the character's concerns at the center of your awareness. Surrender to the character's needs. Commit your energy to fulfilling the character's objectives, thus allowing your own doubts and fears to be over-shadowed by the character's concerns. Relish the character's success and thrill to the character's joy. Actor-produced physical stress will dissolve, leaving your muscles free to respond to the character's circumstances. Remember, actor-tension can prevail only when you lose your concentration, drop out of character, and involve yourself in actor problems. (More about this in Parts II and III.)

Don't Lose Sight Of Your Goal

A soldier encased in heavy and cumbersome body armor made of chain mail, or plate, is slow, clumsy and inflexible. An actor encased in mental armor is in much the same state psychologically and physically. Relaxation techniques, therefore, are as important as any of the work you do to improve your craft. But, don't lose your perspective. If you obsess over relaxation, you are a little like the cat who learned his tail was happiness, so he drove himself mad chasing his tail.

Without a doubt, you want to rid yourself of actor-anxiety. If you are driven by your own fears, you can't be in character. Some actors, however, seem to make relaxation the final goal, rather than a means to the end. The results are no improvement over the work of the tense actor. In one instance, we get the nervous actor who is so self-obsessed that nothing happens. In the other instance, we get the comatose actor who is relaxed, yet boring.

Another example of obsession with relaxation is the performer who doesn't get cast because the moment before the audition becomes a sideshow. I am referring to actors who request a moment before they begin work, then perform lengthy and elaborate rituals before performing. First, they go through a relaxation routine to eliminate their anxieties and physical tension. Perhaps they do breathing exercises. Next, they perform calisthenics to pump up the energy. Then, they go through another complicated procedure to assume the character-anxieties. Possibly, they take another moment to do sensory work. I have watched these actors audition and they have no idea how put off the auditor is by being forced to sit through the actor's homework.

Practice relaxation techniques and sharpen your concentration skills until you can shift seamlessly from actor-concerns to character-concerns. Hone these skills, until you can slip, invisibly, into the character's skin. I have always appreciated the advice I once heard attributed to the distinguished film actor, Spencer Tracy who starred in such classics as *Inherit The Wind*, and *Judgment At Nuremberg*. The advice simply stated is: "Acting is great. Just don't get caught at it." An efficient way to avoid getting caught acting is to make a smooth and subtle transition into your work.

Without reliable relaxation techniques, you have little probability of becoming a successful actor. As long as your fears run you, you are a victim of your own thoughts. You can learn to relax in the same way you hone your other basic skills. Master fundamental techniques and practice them until they become second nature.

EXERCISES

Note that you are advised to do most of these exercises sitting or standing rather than lying down. You won't do much acting lying down and you want to be able to relax in the state in which you'll be working.

EASY BREATHING

Sit or stand, with your feet fairly close together, in a relaxed but erect position. Keep your spine comfortably straight. Drop your shoulders and be sure your back isn't arched. Notice your breathing. Do not interfere with your breath—simply pay attention to the inhalation and exhalation. Are you breathing through your mouth or your nose? Is your breathing deep or shallow, fast or slow? Explore ways to make your breath interesting enough to hold your attention. For instance, in your mind's eye, see the air coming in and going out. To sustain this image, you might try coloring your breath. Try breathing in one color and breathing out another. You may find it more effective to focus on the kinesthetic experience. Feel your rib cage expand and contract. Experience the various muscles that are involved in the process. Perhaps if you imagine the inhalation and exhalation producing sounds, such as music, that will improve your concentration. Listen to the musical notes as you inhale, then exhale them. Use your imagination and experiment.

When your mind wanders, don't chastise yourself. Instead, gently re-direct your attention to your breath. Continue to observe your breathing for five to ten minutes.

BREATH COUNTING

Focus on your breath (see "Easy Breathing") and count exhalations. Count to four, then begin again. You may find it helpful to add "and" on the inhalation. Do not alter your breathing; simply count exhalations for five to ten minutes.

DEEP BREATHING

Take a deep breath through your nostrils and slowly exhale through your mouth. When you think you have completed the exhalation, exhale some more until you are sure you have emptied your lungs. Hold for five to ten seconds, then allow your lungs to fill naturally. Repeat these steps three or four times.

MEASURED BREATHING

Sit quietly for a few moments and observe your normal breathing. You probably inhale quite a bit longer than you exhale which causes you to retain carbon-dioxide. Change the ratio. Inhale for two seconds, hold the breath for four seconds, then exhale for four seconds. Repeat this breathing pattern for two or three minutes.

BREATHE INTO THE TENSION

Direct your attention to a part of your body where you are most tense. Imagine breathing into those muscles. Visualize the soothing air releasing all the tension. Imagine the air giving the muscles a massage, or relaxing the muscles with a deep heat. Feel the air kneading and stroking your neck, back, or shoulders. Spend as much time as you need to smooth out all the knots.

Body INVENTORY

Lie on the floor with your back comfortably flat and your hands on your abdomen. Bend your knees and bring your feet toward your body until they are resting comfortably, soles flat on the floor. Close your eyes if you wish. Direct your awareness to your feet, first your left one, and clearly imagine your toes. Scan your toes for tension. If they are tense, imagine sending a soothing breath to the taut muscles, then feel your toes relax. (See "Breathe Into The Tension.") Move your awareness to the rest of your foot and gradually up your leg. Stop and check for tension in your foot, ankle, calf, knee, and so on up to your hip. Release any tension before you move from one spot to another. Scan your right leg in the same manner. Now move your awareness to your trunk, then slowly up your body toward your head and finally out to your fingertips.

Take your time, especially in the areas where you habitually hold tension. Release any tight muscles before you continue with the inventory. Don't forget to scan your face in detail, noting the areas around the eyes and mouth for example. When you complete your inventory, enjoy your relaxed state for a few minutes before you slowly open your eyes, stretch, wriggle around a bit, move your arms and legs and get up slowly. Experiment with this exercise while seated.

PRACTICE, PRACTICE, PRACTICE

Regular repetition of these exercises will help you establish a benchmark, or reference point, so you can recognize and reduce inappropriate physical tension. If fear has paralyzed you, do some relaxation work and get back on track. Like any of the exercise programs in this book, these models will work for you only if you repeat them frequently. Occasional practice, when you are desperate, won't do you much good.

If you have serious problems with physical tension, you might want to investigate some books on this subject. Try: Herbert Benson's *The Relaxation Response, Stress Without Distress* by Hans Selye, or *Less Stress In 30 Days* by Gillespie and Bechtel. Lawrence LeShan's book, *How To Meditate* also will help you learn to concentrate and relax.

Look into Hatha Yoga or biofeedback. Check the library and bookstores for guided relaxation on audio tape.

Notice that all the techniques for learning to relax depend upon strong powers of concentration. Each requires you to: (1) steer your mind away from thoughts that made you tense, and (2) focus your attention on a particular task that does not naturally fascinate you. If you have not mastered concentration, these exercises will help sharpen this skill.

The difficulty in life is the choice.
George Moore,
The Bending of the Bough, Act III

Exploring The Script

Detective Work

Things are seldom what they seem,
Skim milk masquerades as cream.
William S. Gilbert,
H.M.S. Pinafore

Exploring The Script

Detective Work

Y ou can save yourself a considerable amount of work if you learn how to read your script the first time you pick it up. There is a temptation to attack the material, as though it were an enemy to be vanquished. You may think you should begin immediately to analyze the scenes and make decisions about how to play the character. Instead, suspend your critical faculties momentarily and read the script the way you read a novel. Cast yourself in the role you are going to play—just as you would cast yourself in the role of the central character in a novel you are reading for entertainment. Allow yourself to experience the events and to hear the other characters' dialogue as if the individuals were speaking to you. The purpose of this read-through is to awaken your unconscious to the possibilities of the character's experience. With this approach, you will store impressions and gather intuitive knowledge. Once you have begun your detective work (exploring the script), you are relying more on the use of your critical faculties. It will never be possible to return to the point of absolute innocence you enjoyed when you first picked up the script. Take advantage of this state of innocence.

Play Detective, Before You Play The Character

When you have completed your first reading of the script, it is time to put on your detective hat. Play sleuth and sift through the piece, finding the building blocks you will need to construct a launching pad for your character. In the following chapters, we will look at questions you pose to yourself, as the character. Using these questions, you will probe the script for:

1. The context in which the scene occurs (the given circumstances)
2. What happens (the dramatic action)
3. The revelations that occur (new information revealed during the action)

In some instances, the clues that allow you to answer your questions will be fairly apparent; in others, you will need to do some clever detective work. Occasionally, you will fill in blanks based on only the slightest hints from the writer. The following suggestions should point you toward an expedient method of exploration. Then, each chapter in this section provides directions for a particular search.

A Little Objectivity Goes A Long Way

When you begin the exploration keep in mind that its purpose is to give you, the character, more to think about—it must *not* give you, the actor, more to think about. You want to set the character's mind in motion—your actor-mind will not need stimulation. Do the script exploration in first person, not third person. Don't waste time with "Her brother is dying"; instead, go immediately to the character's thought process with "*My* brother is dying." Begin at once to think of *my* problems and *my* needs, not *hers* or *his*. Since you must eventually accept that these events are happening to you, why cover the same ground twice?

Not only is thinking in third person a waste of valuable time and energy, it will build a wall between you and the character. If you think of the events as happening to *him* or *her*, you will be directing yourself to observe the action from a safe distance. You will be encouraged, then, to function as a critic rather than a doer. In defense, you may say you need perspective and objectivity for accuracy, but that part of the process is easy. Besides, your character doesn't need an analyst—your character needs a body, a heart, a mind, and a soul. Use your exploration to involve yourself in your character's problems, thus evoking your intuition.

Some dreadful acting is done by actors who excel at script dissection and discussion. The process of exploring the script should be a way of involving yourself in the character's problems, not an excuse to merely psychoanalyze the character. Your goal is to get inside the character's skin, not the skin of the character's psychiatrist, counselor, minister, or best friend. It is more important to know what your character needs and does, than to know what your character is "like."

When an actor describes what his character is "like," he makes comments such as: "This guy is really mixed-up. He loves his wife and wants what's best for her, still he just can't bring himself to give up the gambling." If the actor stops there, he doesn't know anymore about this man than the fellow's friends know and it's impossible to truthfully play this information. What the actor *can* use to get inside the character's mind is: "Of course, I love my wife—I married her, didn't I? And I try to be a good provider, but I'm entitled to a little fun, aren't I? After all, I'm the one out there breaking my back trying to earn a buck. She doesn't believe that my luck is turning—but I can feel it." Use your analysis to get into your character's mind (so you can experience the character's needs and think the character's thoughts), not just to understand your character.

Avoid Playing The Judge

You don't need to approve of the character you portray—you might not choose to live with a person like him/her or want your children to turn out this way. You do need, however, to see the action on-stage strictly from the character's point of view. One minute after the curtain goes down on the final performance you may acknowledge that the character is despicable or unspeakably stupid. Nevertheless, while playing the role you must commit yourself to the character's needs, embrace his or her belief system, and work with his or her physical, mental and emotional "equipment." If you indulge in judging the character, you will be prepared to show us what you think of the character—that isn't the same thing as *revealing* the character. Your job is to illuminate the character. Let the audience do the judging. By playing the character well you imply neither endorsement nor condemnation of the character's qualities and actions.

Be equally wary of judging the material. If you think a script is boring, you may be overlooking vital information. Perhaps you haven't explored the script carefully enough, or perhaps you are avoiding the emotional content. Judging the material allows you to justify a cowardly decision to abandon the role of the *doer* and escape to the more comfortable role of critic. Becoming the critic is a sure-fire method for disengaging yourself from the action and deserting the character.

Keep in mind that, during script exploration, your goal is to turn up interesting and stimulating information. You are looking for facts that help you establish guidelines and spark your imagination. You are discovering possibilities, not a list of rigid rules that will govern your behavior. You are establishing a framework within which you can let the part play you.

Circumstances alter cases.
Charles Dickens,
Mystery of Edwin Drood IX

The web of our life is of a mingled yarn,
good and ill together.
William Shakespeare, *All's Well that
Ends Well*, Act IV, Scene 3, Line 83

CHAPTER 7

Defining The Given Circumstances

Daydreaming And Sleuthing

Imagine it is a clear, sunny day in spring. You just got the news that one of your most heartfelt dreams has been realized, and you are entering a familiar room filled with close, supportive friends. Everything that happens next will be filtered through this particular set of circumstances: the pleasant weather, the uplifting news, and the camaraderie of agreeable company. You will see faces, hear conversations, taste food and beverages, smell fragrances, and feel the textures in your surroundings through the set of filters created by this particular context. Every moment of every day you exist in a specific set of given circumstances. Every moment of your life owes its unique qualities to the events that preceded it, the physical setting, the interpersonal relationships in operation, and your particular view of life.

Let's replay our scenario. This time, you trudge through snow and slush to a place you have never before seen. You just got devastating news. Most of the people here are strangers to you, and the one person you do know isn't likely to sympathize with your misfortune. The *frame* for the ensuing events has been drastically altered. New filters are in place. In a sense, your field of view has been altered. Everything you see, hear, taste, smell and touch will be colored by the new context. You have never yet experienced an event that was not part of a complex set of given circumstances. Don't ask your character to do what is humanly impossible.

You cannot expect your character to appear human without an inner life. This inner life, or core, is a web of memories, expectations, life lessons, fears and dreams. Clearly, the experiences of the past shape that core. By defining your character's particular past, therefore, you provide the context that shapes your character's inner life. You did not spring to life one day with a fully developed personality. Your disposition, while already unique in infancy, was further molded by your experiences. Just as the elements of your given circumstances helped to define your inner being, so do the elements of your character's world shape his or her spirit.

Provide your character a unique and specific world, or context. That context includes the physical setting, the personal relationships, events that occurred before the scene begins, as well as the attitudes shaped by those events. These elements compose not only the framework within which the action of the scene takes place, they also provide the springboard or impetus for the ensuing events. By forging this framework you propel your character into action.

Ask The Right Questions

As you examine the script, some facts pertaining to your character's given circumstances will seem to jump off the page. In other cases, you may have to dig for answers, tenaciously pursuing vague hints. It may take considerable imagination, even research, to answer some questions, because the script seems to offer no clues. In some instances, you will fill in your own experiences. Keep your purpose in mind: you are providing a filter to which you can commit as being truthful. The goal is not *correct* choices. After all, if you were to interview twelve actors, all of whom had played a classic role, you might get twelve different answers to some of these questions. Furthermore, just because you commit to one answer today that doesn't mean it becomes the only choice available to you. Your answers are far from being written in stone. They are possibilities you plan to explore. Don't cripple your imagination by demanding perfect answers.

While it is important to avoid the trap of seeking perfect answers, it is equally important to be specific. Don't plunk your poor character into a nebulous *sort of* world. Create a world of substance. Make your answers concrete, detailed and unique. It is one thing to decide that you, the character, blame your father because he wasn't there to be your parent. It is another to relive, through *remember when's*, a few of the specific moments from your past that support your conviction. Your assessment of your father takes on new meaning if you recall in vivid detail the day you and your brother were shipped off to an aunt's house. You see your father through different eyes after reliving the endless days you spent hoping for phone calls and letters that never came. You fill your character's inner mind with reality if you recall the first Christmas in the foster home after your aunt passed away. You will view your father's actions from a particular viewpoint if you call up vivid images of the humiliations you endured in the foster home.

Define your character's world by answering the following questions for him or her:

◆ *Who am I?*
Consider job (i.e., how you spend your days), age, educational background, economic status, religious background, physical attributes, your goals in life, etc. The more detailed your answer, the richer your work. You are creating the lens through which you, as the character, will view the world. For example, a person with strong religious convictions is likely to view death differently from an agnostic. A police officer and a card shark, each viewing the same event, are apt to have two different interpretations of the behavior.

◆ *Who am I talking to?*
Ask the same type of questions you asked for *Who am I?* about the other people in the scene. Be certain to identify their jobs and define your relationship with them. Your past experiences with an individual are bound to color the present. Clarify the power dispersal in the relationship. A reaction you feel free to externalize with one person may get you in hot water with someone else. Anchor the characters in action. You know the individuals by their actions. What have they done to you? Recreate, in your mind's eye, important events you have shared with the people in the scene.

After you establish your literal relationship to the other people, define what they represent to you. For example, if the other character is my boss, I know that she has a lot to do with my economic future. Perhaps it is even more significant, however, that—on an emotional level—I am still dealing with my mother who told me I would never succeed.

◆ *Who are the people we talk about?*
Use the questions for *Who am I?* and *Who am I talking to?*

◆ *Where am I?*
Define the physical space, i.e., size, shape, colors, textures, temperature, light, etc. What do people do in this place? What is your relationship to the space? What have you done here? How familiar is it to you? Is it your turf, or someone else's? If you are in someone else's territory, what is your relationship to the owner or owners? What has happened to you here, or what do you imagine might happen? Is this a place in which you have experienced humiliation, or a place where you triumphed over a formidable enemy? Is this a place where you have played silly games or fought serious emotional battles to their bitter conclusions?

◆ *What are the places we refer to?*
Use questions similar to those in *Where am I?*

◆ *What time is it?*
Determine the year, time of day, time of year. See, hear, taste, touch and smell your answers—the special colors of dawn, the crisp chill of an autumn day, the let-down of the day after Christmas. Clarify the Zeitgeist, or the spirit of the time in which your character lives. The experiences and outlooks characteristic of one period or generation may contrast sharply with those of another. If you are an unwed and pregnant young woman in the 1930's, abortion is not the option in the same way it would be to a character at the end of the twentieth century.

◆ *What are the events we refer to?*
Fill in specific details and bring to life the events mentioned, or implied. Visit in your imagination, those moments. Recall, in vivid details the actions of particular individuals. (For help using *remember when's,* refer to Chapter 2.)

◆ *What happened to me in the moment before the scene?*
Recreate the events that occurred immediately before the first moment in the scene. A dry description of the events is useless. That would only serve to provide an intellectual explanation, and it is not likely to motivate any doing. It is one thing to decide, "Someone said hateful things to me before I walked in the room." It is quite another to see, in your mind's eye, the specific individual and hear, in your mind's

ear, the words spoken to you. If, in addition, the speaker is someone from your real life, and the words are close to those that have previously wounded you, you will have activated your emotional engine and catapulted yourself into action.

◆ *What is my point of view, or how do I think the world works?*
For example:
- "Human beings are inherently good, and ultimately the human spirit will triumph over evil."
- "I worked hard for what I have, and I don't plan to share it with anyone."

This question is critical. After all, when you determine your point of view—what you assume is true about the way the world works—you are establishing a belief system, a framework in which you, the character, operate. We all have belief systems and each of those beliefs is anchored in specific action. Our convictions are inspired by, and supported by, particular events in our lives. For example, if you believe that all women or men are unfaithful, it is because of *lessons* you learned. Perhaps you were deeply hurt by someone who was unfaithful to you or to someone you loved (probably a parent). The pain you suffered because of that infidelity taught you a lesson. Every aspect of your outlook on life is directly linked to events you experienced. You may not recall the event that originally established the belief system; nevertheless, you do remember events that corroborate the point of view.

Find your character's point of view, and anchor it in action by identifying the specific events in your character-life that have shaped your outlook. If you relive, in your imagination, an event that taught you this belief, you will internalize the belief and avoid posturing. Your character does not *choose* to embrace these beliefs; your character has learned by experience that this is how the world works. **A point of view is something you believe, something you internalize—not something you can play—and it must be anchored in action.**

Substitutions

Your real-life given circumstances may bear little resemblance to those of your character. Therefore, you will need to use a combination of imagination and substitution to find where the character's circumstances and yours intersect. It is not enough to understand the character's context. You must be willing to identify with that context on a deep and personal level.

Imagine the actor who is playing Ann in Arthur Miller's *All My Sons*. The actor is answering: *Who are the people we talk about?* Ann talks about her father and her first fiancé, who is dead. The actor must have specific images in her mind of actual people when she says those lines. If she fails to substitute, or plug in, actual people to play those roles, she may falter. She will have to talk about broad, and therefore vague, concepts of *fiancé* or *father* and the lines will be flat.

If, in contrast, she *casts* people she knows in these roles, much of her work is done for her. She may cast her real-life father or she may substitute a father-figure. Subsequently, as the actor speaks—in character—about her father, images of the actor's experiences with the substituted individual will dance in her mind. The images create nuances of meaning far more subtle than anything an actor could engineer. The actor need not have lost a *fiancé* during wartime, but she must find in her own experience a corresponding loss. She must then be willing to let the two experiences—hers and the character's—meld. She must be willing to reopen her own wound and add to that loss the particular facts of Ann's loss. Imagination makes it possible to fuse the two histories and produce a new one that is unique to Ann but still intensely personal for the actor.

Substitutions are also invaluable when establishing your character's point of view. Your character may have goals or fears that have no emotional heat for you. Recently I watched an actor in one of my classes agonize as he attempted to identify with the needs of a character whose primary motivation was a trunk load of drug money. The suffering actor complained, "I just can't seem to care about the money. Never in my life have I made a decision in which money was the primary consideration." I asked him to play the scene substituting a lead role in a new Spielberg film for the money. From the moment the scene began, the actor fully dedicated himself to the action. Keep in mind that, in a situation such as this one, the audience neither knows, nor cares, whether you are thinking about the money or a film role. They only care whether you play the action of the scene. When you commit your psychic and physical energy to actions that are congruent with the character's story, the audience will simply follow the action. They don't *pick* at your performance, trying to catch you at using your own needs to motivate action.

Using substitutions for *Who am I talking to?* is a valuable technique. I caution you, however, to avoid a mistake commonly made by actors using this process. For instance, if you are playing Chris, another character in *All My Sons*, you might substitute your own father for Joe. You shouldn't, however, focus on sustaining a mental image of your real father, because this diversion will disconnect you from the interchange of action with the actor playing Joe. If the mental image of your father becomes your chief concern, your inner dialogue will cease to reflect character-thoughts. You will, instead, have a conversation with yourself in which you repeat actor-thoughts. "I have to remember that this is my father. I have to hear my father's voice. Oh, no, I lost the image of my father's face—I have to get it back."

Struggling to sustain the relationship between the past and the present doesn't work because it is unnatural behavior. In real life, we constantly experience events during which our unconscious mind makes substitutions. For example, while a teacher critiques your work, you may, on an unconscious level, respond to memories of your father's criticism. Notice that in the real-life instance you never *try* to recall your father criticizing you. On the contrary, because your mental images of past events are so vivid, the current events automatically trigger the memories. The situation, the teacher's words and facial expressions, the setting—all these elements activate recall of images.

Return to our example in which you are playing Chris. You must create the connection between your character's father, Joe, and your own father. Solidify the link with specific actions—that is always the *glue* that makes substitutions stick. Connect the actions to dialogue in your scene. Take, for example, the moment when you say, "Dad, you killed twenty-one men!"[1] In addition to the other work you have done to fill that line with meaning, you could use those words to link Joe to your real-life father. Recall a time when your father let you down. Clearly, you don't need to refer to a situation where your father's actions led to someone's death. What matters most is that you find a time when you felt betrayed by your father and deeply disappointed in him. You could use a situation where you felt your father's actions were hurtful to innocent people. When you have found the juncture where your experience and that of the character meet, you can trust your preparation to fill the moment. You have woven the words and actions of your father together with the words and actions of Chris's father. When you hear Joe's lines, you can expect them to set off psychological tremors.

To successfully use substitutions, remember these two caveats: **(1) You must trust your character's memory of events that you have imagined for him or her. (2) You must trust that the appropriate mental images will be automatically triggered by the events that occur in the character's present moments.**

EXERCISES

Keep these guidelines in mind as you practice the exercises:

☞ **Remember to work in first person.**
Discover *your* problems and needs, not *his* or *her* problems. Don't talk about the character from a safe, objective point of view.

☞ **Focus on events.**
Your history is composed of specific events. Concern yourself with what *happened* in your imaginary past.

☞ **Don't be tempted to go for the emotions.**
The feelings are a result of what happened. Don't get lost in an attempt to find the *correct* emotions.

☞ **Make choices that matter.**
Steer away from mundane events that don't interest or affect you. Create incidents that were infuriating, devastating, hilarious, tragic, shocking, terrifying, revolting or inspiring.

☞ **Pack some emotional baggage.**
Most of us carry around considerable garbage resulting from unresolved issues with our parents. Provide your character with similar emotional baggage; it furnishes excellent fuel. You may be able to select appropriate details from your own history and use them *as is,* or you may need to embellish your experiences.

☞ **Be specific.**
The more specifics you add to the world in which the action occurs, the richer your work will be. Everything that happens occurs in a specific environment. Every event you experience in real life has a direct, or indirect, connection to all the events in your past. Your interpretation of what goes on around you is colored by what you have already done and what has been done to you. A character without a past has amnesia. Are you certain that is the character you want to portray?

☞ **Be a clever detective.**

The answers to your questions are either clearly illustrated or implied in the dialogue and the details come from your imagination. Test the logic of your discoveries against the requirements of the script.

☞ **See, hear, taste, feel and smell your answers.**

Generalities are only useful as a starting point. The only answers that will have genuine impact on your work are those you image—you must see, hear, taste, feel, and smell your choices. The most detailed and intelligent answers won't work, if they don't involve you or if they don't evoke feelings. Writing a biography for the character is a waste of good paper if you write as though you were referring to someone else. Unless you record what happened as if it happened to you, and unless you relive the events in your imagination, the work is a pointless exercise. It's a waste of time to dredge up complicated explanations of people, places and events. You must, through your imagination, *visit* your character's past.

☞ **Imagination is the key.**

Your imagination will enable you to bring those experiences to life. You will reproduce some of your own images and you will create new images. You will produce the new images in several ways. You may recombine mental pictures from your own real life experiences. In some cases, you may draw upon images resulting from vicarious experiences. You have a storehouse of these images from books, movies, plays, television, and stories you have heard.

☞ **Take your time.**

Feel your way through this exploration. Daydream the character's life into existence. Don't rush.

☞ **Have fun.**

I've never understood why some actors regard this process as work. This is to me as much fun as the performing. Free yourself to privately indulge in the make-believe world of your character and you strengthen your confidence in your ability to live there publicly.

START AT HOME

Define your own given circumstances.

PRACTICE MAKES PERFECT

Choose a character in a script for practice purposes and imagine that person's world. Don't wait until you have an acting assignment to test the questions that will help you define your character's given circumstances.

BEING THERE

Choose a scene and layer in the specifics to define one element of your character's given circumstances. For example, knowing that the little girl you talk about in the scene is your adopted daughter is only the beginning of your preparation. Relive some key moments with her, perhaps her first Christmas with you. Create the event in graphic detail. Your mind and body respond to specifics, not to generalities.

- Do you hear the Christmas music that was playing that morning?
- See, in your mind's eye, her dress: the color of the fabric, the shape of the collar, the sash around her waist, the ruffle at the hem.
- Savor the taste of the chocolate cream you were eating.
- Visualize the tremble of the little girl's lips when she saw the doll you bought her.
- Feel, again, the shy hug she gave you when she murmured, "Thank you."

Focus on what each of you did; don't catalogue or analyze emotions. If you recreate that morning in sufficient detail by seeing, hearing, smelling, tasting and touching your way through the events, you get inside the character. When you play the scene, each moment between you and the other characters will reverberate off the events of that Christmas morning.

Some actors ignore the given circumstances because they don't regard the character's context critical. Besides, they don't find doing the detective work nearly so exciting as deciding, "How should I feel when I say that line?" Other actors determine the given circumstances, but for the wrong reasons. They complete the work for the purpose of getting *right* answers; or, they worry about being caught in a mistake by the director, the audience, or—God forbid—a critic. Those actors are apt to become hopelessly entangled in the preparation maze. They become victims of *paralysis by analysis.*

Defining your character's world should set you free to work in a creative state; it shouldn't send you into an intellectual, emotional and physical shut-down. Answering these questions should silence your inner critic and propel you into action. If you define your character's world, you can get into your character-mind and out of your actor-mind. If you get inside your character's mind, you can listen with your heart as well as your head. This work prepares you to hear, see, taste, touch, and smell the events of the scene as though they were happening to you, the character, not you, the actor. In real life, your given circumstances dramatically affect you, but—because that has always been so—you may not be aware of it. Your behavior is deeply influenced by the physical setting, your relationship with the other people, your point of view, and—most of all—your moment, and moments, before. Give your character the benefit of a similarly complex web of circumstances.

Remember these pointers to maximize the usefulness of the given circumstances. **(1) When defining your character's world, give yourself choices filled with vivid detail and link them closely enough to your own experience to provide emotional heat. (2) While playing, direct your physical and mental energies toward solving the character's problems.** If you fulfill these objectives, you can safely expect that those choices will surface in your work. Trust.

FOOTNOTES

[1]Arthur Miller, *All My Sons* (New York: Dramatists Play Service, Inc., 1947) p. 58. Copyright, Arthur Miller, 1947.

O, speak to me no more;
these words, like daggers, enter in mine ears.
William Shakespeare, *Hamlet*,
Act III, sc. 4, line 94

CHAPTER 8

DISCOVERING THE DRAMATIC ACTION

Who Is Doing What To Whom

UNDERSTANDING ACTION

Action adventure movies are filled with dramatic action, but so is a Chekhov play. The action movie involves mainly physical activity—lots of chase scenes, car crashes and explosions. In contrast, the Chekhov piece consists mostly of psychological action—emotional explosions and clashing of wills. In either case, the characters are *doing* and the plot consists of a series of events. The action in the movie is obvious to the most casual observer. An effective production of the play, however, demonstrates that even people who are relatively still can be in full action, since dramatic action is mental as well as physical.

ACTION IS DOING

Dramatic action involves people *doing* things to one another—people giving and receiving, exchanging energy. There can be no action without acting and reacting. *The American College Dictionary* gives these definitions for *react*: (1) "to act in a reverse direction or manner," (2) "to act in opposition, as against some force," and (3) "to respond to a stimulus in a particular manner." The *Roget's Thesaurus* lists these synonyms: "respond, reverberate, return, echo, boomerang, backfire, recoil and fly back." All these words describe *doing* or action. They evoke images of contests, power struggles, tension, competition, interaction, conflict.

When the action is physical, we recognize it easily. I push you—you push back. I pat you soothingly—you respond by moving closer, jerking away, or tensing up to shut me out. When the action is mental, it is more subtle yet still forceful. If I use my words to bathe you with admiration, you may glow with acknowledgment, and reflect back some of the warmth on me. In another instance, you may be embarrassed and decline the appreciation—as though it were a gift too expensive for the occasion. In response to the last two illustrations, you may insist that you are "just listening." Still you are listening in a particular way. For example, if while you listen, you send me waves of polite refusal, that is your action or doing. Your listening, or doing, consists of processing my message, assimilating information, lining up the new data with old data, reaching conclusions and adjusting accordingly. You are very active.

Every speech in your script is packed with dramatic action. A speech several lines long may contain several actions. Let's examine one line of an imagined exchange to demonstrate the range of possibilities. Perhaps my line is: "Don't worry, I'll take care of that." I could use those words to rescue you. If you are listening, you will experience the impact of my words and respond to the stimulus with a reciprocal action. You might respond by using "I can take care of it myself" to thank me, reassure me, or humor me. I could just as well have used my line to shame you, threaten you, or charm you. You might, then, use your line to dismiss me, belittle me, insult me, or silence me. In each of these examples the words convey a message. The passing of messages is the doing. I am doing and you are reacting or acting in opposition, as against a force. We are giving and receiving.

ACTION INVOLVES CHANGE

Imagine you have just noticed a snow globe. You probably won't be interested in the globe so long as the snow remains on the ground undisturbed. Your impulse is to upset this miniature universe. You create chaos by sending the snow flying through the air, then watch, fascinated, by the action of the snow falling back to the ground. It is human nature to be more fascinated by matters unsettled than by those resolved. In the same way, audiences are more fascinated by change than by constancy.

When people interact, give and receive, or exchange energies, changes take place. The changes might include power shifts, changes of heart, reorganization of alliances, and reversals of fortune. Perhaps the changes involve recognition of betrayal, deviation from a course, a switch in tactics, or shifts of attention. The possibilities are endless, but some degree of change is essential.

An audience rapidly loses interest when there are no changes, when nothing happens. We expect the curtain to come down when all the issues are resolved, the struggles are over, the battles have been won, and the *dust has settled*. If a scene begins, continues, then ends and everything and everyone remain exactly as they were in the beginning, there was no action. If there was no struggle, no negotiation, no seduction, no case won or lost, no love shared or withheld, the audience lost interest. Sometimes the action, or the changes are subtle—barely discernible. Sometimes they are bold and bring down the rafters. But without action there is no drama. We associate change with animate beings—with what is alive. When we think of the opposite of change, we think of inanimate objects, or what is no longer alive. Take care that the audience does not mistake you for a piece of the furniture.

Action Comes Out Of Need

Action arises out of need. If I have everything I need why should I *do* anything? I am picturing myself comfortably languishing in the backyard hammock, cooled by a gentle breeze, shaded by a friendly tree, with the lemonade close at hand. It is a vacation day so I have no appointments, the phone is quiet and the only sounds I hear are birds chirping and squirrels chattering. Why move? Why do anything? Only a need will produce action. If the sun moves far enough that the sun is in my eyes; if the breeze stops or grows too cool; or if I run out of lemonade—I may act. I will do something to fulfill my need. While characters without needs may talk *at* one another, they do not interact. They interact, exchange, give and receive only when they have needs.

Identifying The Action

Identify your character's action by asking the right questions. **Pose the questions *as the character*, not as the actor talking *about* the character.** Talking about the character as *him* or *her* will cause you to distance yourself from the character's needs. Create an instant connection to the character by phrasing all your choices in first person.

After I've watched a scene that didn't work, I often quiz the actors to get a sense of what went wrong. One of my favorite questions is: What happens in this scene? Sometimes the reply clarifies why the scene didn't work. "Well, not much happens really. It's just these two people talking about ...." No! Those characters are driven by needs and those words are tools the characters use to do things to each other that they hope will fulfill their needs. This is what should be happening in the scene. After all, if nothing happens, why would I want to spend my time watching?

Find The Psychic Itch

The first question is: What is my intention or what do I want? Ask yourself what you need to have happen. That is, what would make you feel satisfied, relieved or triumphant? In some scenes, you will find your need by asking: What must I get from the other characters? In other cases, you need to focus on questions such as these: What do I want to offer the other person? What do I want the other person to know? What am I trying to save someone from? Ask yourself: "What is my dilemma?" "What is missing?" "What is this nagging sense of incompleteness that irritates me." I urge my actors to think of the need as the character's *psychic itch*. When an itch exists, a response is involuntary. When your character has a *psychic itch*, you won't need to fabricate the doing.

Take, for example, a scene in which you quarrel with your older brother (your business partner) over a business deal. You insist this deal will make both you and your brother rich, nonetheless your brother doesn't want to become involved with someone who is rumored to be part of the Mafia. You want your brother to sign the contract—that is your objective. In a different scene, you may be trying to get information from the character with whom you are talking. Perhaps that individual knows where the money is buried, who did it, or when the bad guys will get here.

In many scenes, what you are trying to get is less concrete. You may be aiming for acknowledgment, approval or agreement. Perhaps you are asking for mercy, understanding or a pledge of loyalty. You may crave explanations, gratitude or sexual favors. In other cases, you are offering something to the other person. Maybe you are trying to amuse a friend or cheer a loved one. You may want to give solace to a victim of misfortune or congratulations on a job well done. Perhaps you want to deliver an apology or undying devotion. The possibility for variety of wants is endless. Whatever the case, the need represents your dissatisfaction with the status quo. You want things that you do not have. Your mind's eye must be filled with images of people behaving as you would like them to, or circumstances changing.

Guidelines For Identifying The *Psychic Itch*

As you search for the *psychic itch* keep in mind these helpful guidelines:

☛ **Your intention must be on-stage.**
Your intention shouldn't include the audience. For example, if you decide that you want to show how clever you are at dealing with your brother, that is almost certainly an actor-need, not a character-need. Unless there are other people present for whom your character is grandstanding, your character doesn't want to *show* anything to anyone. Your character wants to solve his or her problem.

☛ **Keep it simple.**
Some actors, cast as the younger sibling in the contract scene, reject the obvious intention. They don't commit to persuading the brother to sign the contract because they mistrust an objective, or need, that is so evident. Those actors waste valuable time digging for a complicated and obscure intention.

☛ **Commit to some objectives that are doomed to failure.**
You may question the obvious intention protesting that it doesn't make sense. "Why should I commit to convincing my brother to sign the contract when I can see that in the end he refuses?" If your acting is to resonate with life-energy, you must be willing to do just that. Besides, your character doesn't know how this conversation is going to end. Don't spoil the suspense for the audience by forecasting the conclusion.

It's tempting to avoid commitment to an intention that guarantees you will experience failure. No one enjoys failing. Nevertheless if you insist on committing without exception to character-needs that are realized, you will eliminate effort and conflict. Indeed, what most holds the audience's attention is the character's struggle to accomplish challenging objectives.

☛ **Focus on immediate needs.**
Concentrate on character needs that require immediate attention. While intentions designed on a grand and global scale may help you understand your character's life

goals, you should choose intentions you can do something about in the next few minutes. It may be helpful to know that ultimately your character hopes to save starving children. All the same, unless there are specific actions you can execute in the next few minutes, committing exclusively to this broad intention will cause you to play generalities.

☛ **At the end of the scene, you should know whether or not you succeeded in your intention.**

If, after playing the scene, you have no idea whether you won or lost, moved closer to your character-goal or totally missed the boat, you probably have chosen an intention that is not playable. You should have a sense of whether the *psychic itch* has been relieved or exacerbated.

☛ **Your character's goal may not make sense.**

Your character's most heartfelt need may be to recapture a lost opportunity, or bring back to life a loved one who died. You may overlook those intentions because they aren't "logical." Take a closer look and remember that much of human behavior doesn't make sense.

☛ **Your wants should make you uncomfortable.**

Perhaps you don't commit to needs that would motivate you to action because experiencing the need makes you uncomfortable. What if your character is deeply ashamed and your action is the unburdening of your soul? You must feel the shame before you can experience the need to rid yourself of the burden. That is one of the perverse facets of acting. You must seek out uncomfortable sensations. The *psychic itch* will motivate you to action, but only if you are willing to itch.

☛ **Your needs should focus your attention outside yourself.**

Where will you get the information that tells you whether you are fulfilling your intention? Be certain you commit to intentions that cause you to monitor the actions, thoughts, and feelings of the other characters. For example, let's say you made this unwise choice: "I want to do a good job of persuading my brother to sign the contract." Where will you look to check your progress, to determine whether you succeed in discharging your obligation? You will watch yourself, right? Even if you commit to "I need to convince him to sign the contract," you are apt to keep a close eye on yourself. Now the point of concentration isn't his signing the contract—it is your powers of persuasion. Rather than studying your brother's behavior to see how close he is to signing the contract, you will scrutinize yourself and your own behavior. That is precisely what you want to avoid.

Commit, instead, to "I need him to sign the contract." Where is your attention now? Whose body language, facial expressions, tone of voice and inflections will give you the information you need to make appropriate changes in your tactics? You need to watch the other character to see whether you are succeeding in your intention, and that is where your attention must be if you are to be truthful in your work. If you spend your energy judging yourself, you will focus on your actor-needs and play your actor-actions. Since actions tell the story, you will tell your actor-story.

Choose your needs carefully to guarantee that you evoke character-action. Only then will you reveal the character's story.

☞ **Your needs should produce responses that you experience in your body.**
State your intention. Perhaps it is: "I need him to sign this contract;" or "I need her to admit that what she did was wrong;" or "I need her to know how much I appreciate her." Do you feel something in your muscles? Does your body respond? If your throat goes dry, your shoulders tense, your stomach lurches, or your heart lifts, this is a choice that has ignited your imagination. If you involuntarily smile, catch your breath, let out a sigh, or clamp your hand over your mouth, this choice is *in your body* and will evoke action. If your knees go weak, your eyes burn, or the muscles in your groin tighten, you have made a productive choice. If your body remains passive, the choice is probably only a mental exercise and it is not likely to be productive. Find an answer that will get the information out of your head and into your body.

☞ **Determine who is in the driver's seat.**
In some scenes, *your* need is the need that drives the action. Refer to the earlier example where you were trying to convince your brother to sign the contract. Without your need there is no scene. Your want sets the action in motion. Assume, on the other hand, that you are playing the brother. Now, your need is to convince your sibling that this punk he wants to deal with is bad news. You want to prevent your impulsive brother from wrecking the company and bringing shame on the family name. Rather than initiating the action, your want is a reaction to your brother's need. If he failed to introduce his need, you might initiate a completely different action with another need. That would be a different scene.

☞ **It's better to have the "wrong" intention than no intention.**
If you complete your investigation and you still feel you don't have the "right" answer, don't despair. The purpose of the search is to stimulate your unconscious, not to determine tidy answers. You may have to work backwards. Pursue the exploration of action *as if* you knew your intention and you may suddenly discover your objective. In some cases, you may not discover your intention until you are on your feet with the scene. Meanwhile, commit to an intention (even if you doubt it is the best one) and stay focused on action. Making conscious choices about needs and creating verbal descriptions of what you may do to satisfy those needs helps to keep your mind focused *on* action and *away* from emotion. (See "First Aid" at the end of this chapter for suggestions if you are stuck.)

The Payoff For Activating The Psychic Itch
Commitment To Needs Breathes Life Into Your Character

Human beings are motivated to action by needs. Make no mistake, you *will* be powered by needs and you *will* be doing. If you don't commit to character-needs, then you will have nothing left to *power the engine* except actor-needs. All your doing, then, will be actor-action and the audience will see only an actor. The audience will have no evidence that your character exists unless you commit to character-needs thus producing character-doing.

When you genuinely commit to the fulfillment of your character-wants, you will automatically dedicate your mind and body to your goal. For example, if you genuinely want your brother to sign the contract, you will, unconsciously, make moment-to-moment adjustments in your actions. You will adapt your doing as the balance of power tilts in your direction or his. Like a heat sensitive rocket, you will aim for the target and adjust your course as you go. You may flatter him; then when he calls you on your tactic, you may shame him, charging him with falsely accusing you. During this interchange of action, you may comfort him, tantalize him, encourage him, threaten him, corner him, shame him, etc.

This relationship between needs and actions, or goals and tactics, is part of your everyday life. You routinely point yourself toward a particular psychological or physical goal, then trust your unconscious to adjust your actions according to the resistance you meet. No doubt, you also make conscious decisions about a course of action. For example, if the contract dispute were a real-life situation, you might plan ahead to flatter your brother, having learned from previous experience that he is susceptible to undue compliments. You may even select an alternative attack in case the flattery fails. Once the exchange begins, however, you will unconsciously adjust your actions to overcome resistance and fulfill your need.

<u>Commitment To Intention Produces Actor-Relaxation</u>

Do you remember the key to relaxation from "Learning To Relax"? We contrasted the results of two directions. First, I asked you to "Show me how you walk," then, "Please bring me the book from the table across the room." The first direction gave you no reason to focus your attention outside yourself and probably caused you to be self-conscious and anxious. In the second case, delivering the book became your *psychic itch*, want, need, intention, or objective. When you committed to that want, you focused your attention outside yourself and your anxiety probably disappeared. If you fill your mind with hunger for your character-want, you won't have time for actor-anxiety. This is specifically why I have urged you make the search for your need more important than finding the *correct* need.

For more help with identifying needs, look at Chapter 9, "I Want You To," in *The Playing Is The Thing*.[1]

SET THE STAKES

The second question is: What are the stakes? What will happen if I fail? What will I gain if I succeed? If I don't get what I want, what will I lose? How will it affect my life? After identifying the need, clarify the intensity of the need. If your character-needs are tepid, the action will probably be insipid and the scene will lack energy. Don't be afraid of melodrama. Why settle for a bland choice such as: "It would be nice to have the extra money this contract would provide." Add emotional heat with this choice: "I owe this guy thousands of dollars. He has hinted that if I return without the signed contract, he will get his money, one way or another. Maybe he is Mafioso. If so, he's sure to have my legs broken, at least—he may have me dumped in the river wearing concrete shoes. My brother has to sign this contract!"

Sometimes the playing is flat because the actors failed to find the action, purpose, desire, and passion in the scene. If this isn't an event that has the potential for profound effect on one or more of the characters, it probably should be a fairly short scene. Otherwise, it is likely to be a dull time for the audience. While you should strive for a kind of truth in art, a presentation of literal everyday life would be deadly boring. An audience craves selective realism. In key confrontational scenes, your character believes: "The next few minutes could change my life." Even in scenes that aren't climactic you must care enough to be touched by what happens and to feel the shift in your fortunes.

Of course, not every scene calls for the highest stakes possible. Indeed, your character would appear quite mad if you forced artificially high stakes into every moment. If you turn every scene into the climax of the piece, you will exhaust and confuse your audience. Out of fear of over-acting, however, many actors consistently set the stakes so low they are virtually non-existent, then wonder why their work is too lifeless to engage the audience.

Bring the character's stakes to life by recalling, in your character-mind, your favorite daydreams and your worst nightmares. In our sample scene, fantasize about handing the signed contract to the shady character and spending freely as the money starts rolling in. On the other hand, recall (as the character) waking up in the middle of the night, bathed in a cold sweat, plagued by nightmares about thugs in dark alleys. Only if the stakes are high enough, will the need turn over your emotional engine.

Obstacles—Don't leave home without them

The third question is: What are the obstacles? If your need, in our sample scene, is to persuade your brother to sign the contract and he is eager to sign it, there is no drama. **The situation becomes dramatic only if there are obstacles in the paths of the characters.** In this scene, your brother's disagreement with you supplies the drama. He represents an obstacle in your path.

It is human nature to avoid obstacles by denying them. It's the "If I ignore them, they'll disappear" game. We've all played it. Nevertheless, during scene exploration, you must inhibit the impulse to deny what is disagreeable. If you fail to place obstacles in your character's path, you eliminate action. Often an actor being quizzed about a scene that isn't working demonstrates how obstacles have been sidestepped. For example, the actor may reply: "Well, I knew he wouldn't sign the contract. I decided that he fights everything I try to do, so I just wanted him to know that I think he's a jerk." I see! You committed to telling him he is a jerk. Tell me what barriers prevent your pronouncement of judgment. What hurdles must you overcome to meet this mind-boggling challenge? I trust that my teasing has made the point that when you choose to merely report on existing conditions, you avoid obstacles and when you avoid obstacles, you eliminate drama. Why would the writer include such a scene?

Guidelines For Identifying The Obstacles

As you identify the obstacles in your character's path, keep in mind these guidelines:

☛ **Don't limit yourself to obvious obstacles.**

Identify both external and internal obstacles. The easiest to identify are the immediate external obstacles: the needs of the other characters or the presence of physical conditions or inanimate objects that act as obstacles. In the scene we are discussing, you need your brother to sign the contract, while he needs you to recognize that signing the contract is not in the best interest of the family. You can't get what you need unless you overcome the immediate obstacle: your brother's objections.

Don't overlook the remote obstacles. Determine how off-stage characters, as well as previous events and circumstances, stand in your way. In a similar scene, a remote obstacle might be the primary roadblock. Let's assume that in the new scenario, your brother wants to sign, yet is reluctant because your father (who is not in the scene) disapproves. In that case, you struggle with your brother, not on the final course of action but, on the best plan for dealing with your father. You respond, then, to both the immediate obstacle of your brother's game plan and the remote obstacle of your father's resistance.

☛ **Some obstacles are internal.**

The struggles most likely to be overlooked are the internal conflicts, or the obstructions within yourself. Allow your character ambivalence and confusion; they will contribute to the chaos that helps to create drama. For instance, at the same time you struggle to persuade your brother to sign the contract, wrestle with your fear that your brother may be right. Perhaps this fellow you want to team up with is dangerous. What if this deal blows up in your face? Maybe you should come clean about your debts, ask your brother for the money to pay the guy off and put this whole thing behind you.

☛ **Layers are important.**

Layer the obstructions in your character's path to make your work rich. In some scenes your character will deal with two or three obvious obstacles, while in another the same character may deal with twenty intricate and subtle difficulties. The more obstacles—both internal and external—your character faces, the more lifelike your work will be. Problems in real life are almost never simple. Remember: a writer captures characters at a crisis point.

Actors often avoid obstacles because they desperately want to be comfortable. Don't fall into this trap. If you play a character who is completely comfortable for long, you probably will bore the audience—they came to see a tug-of-war, contest, struggle, game or competition of some sort. This battle may require a fight to the end with broadaxes or it could be a pillow fight. Perhaps it is a tickling match, a quiet chess game, a spelling bee, or a lazy croquet match on a summer lawn. When all is said and done there must be a reason for action and without obstacles, characters have no reason to act. Name the last play or film you watched, and loved, that focused for a couple of hours on characters effortlessly gliding towards and easily achieving their goals.

DESCRIBING ACTION

VERBS ARE YOUR BEST TOOLS

You will find it helpful to develop a vocabulary for describing dramatic action and verbs are the appropriate tools. There are three types of verbs—each of these being used to describe either an act (*hit*), occurrence (*go*), or state of being (*feel*). An active, or transitive, verb requires an object to complete its meaning. For example, the meaning of the verb *hit* is not complete without an object—a person, animal or thing toward which that action is directed. If I say, "I hit him" or "I hit the car" you will understand my meaning. Should I fail to supply an object for the verb, saying simply "I hit," you can't make sense of my statement. Develop a vocabulary of transitive or active verbs such as: *humiliate, placate, taunt, entrap, corrupt, cuddle, corner, support,* and *tempt.* Since these verbs require a recipient, or object, of your action, they will point you toward *inter*action. If you have thought of the action as *I placate her,* you will be inclined to pay attention to the object of your action. You will direct your energy toward your target and be less likely to "act alone."

Conversely, intransitive verbs tend to detach you from the other characters. Verbs such as *go,* have nothing to do with the other characters and are likely to allow you to proceed unimpeded and without interaction. When you use states of being, such as *I am shy,* to describe what is happening, you are asking for trouble. With that choice, you have assigned yourself to mood patrol. Your job, consequently, is to keep an eye on yourself and make sure that you produce the prescribed state of being. While your shyness in response to an event might provide an amusing, charming, or touching moment, the audience wants to see that discomfort as a reaction, not as the fulfillment of your intention. If we catch you arranging your shyness, we are neither touched, charmed nor amused. Inevitably, it is action that catches our attention. If you engineer shyness, the action we will notice is your manipulation of yourself and the situation. Instead of being charmed or amused, we only wonder why you would think we are so dense as to miss the obvious maneuver.

To insure authenticity in your work, avoid descriptions of action that focus your attention on yourself. Otherwise, you are apt to be self-indulgent, self-aware, or self-judging. In Chapter 14, "Playing The Action," we will discuss producing predetermined results without getting caught acting.

EMOTIONS ARE BY-PRODUCTS, NOT ACTIONS

If you use emotions to describe what is happening, it will set you up to supervise yourself. Focusing on emotional results sends the message to your unconscious that you need to watch yourself to make sure you produce certain feelings. Most actors, when first asked to stop focusing on emotions, are certain that you want to turn them into bloodless marionettes ruled only by intellect. Nothing could be further from the truth. Playing action propels you toward authentic emotions. Feelings are generated when you perform actions. If you, as the character, are consumed by your desire to execute an action, your feelings will change constantly as you succeed or fail. If you are aware of what the other character is doing to you, you will feel the effects of that action. **Emotions are by-products of action.** Read that last sentence again. I have found that once I can get actors to give up the notion that acting is about manipulating their feelings, we are halfway home.

Although words like anger or love serve as transitive verbs, avoid using them to specify action. The trouble is that words describing emotions can also be used as intransitive verbs. Instead, maintain clarity by using the verb that depicts precisely what you would have to do to *anger* or *love* the other person. You might describe the action *love*, for example, with *caress, woo, or adulate*. Emotions are the almost irresistible temptation that stands between most actors and the discovery of action. Resist the siren-song of fickle emotions and fall in love with the dependability of action. Every scene is a story, filled with action both physical and mental, and all the stories go together to tell the longer story—the whole play or film. What the audience most wants from you, as an actor, is for you to shoulder your responsibility in the telling of that story. You fulfill this responsibility by playing the action. In Chapter 15, "Feelings," we will come back to the subject of emotions in your work.

Describe The Moment To Moment Doing

You may find it helpful to score the action in a scene. Experiment with this technique. After you have discovered the given circumstances, go through your script, line by line, deciding what your action might be at each moment. *Might* is the operative word here. Use the scoring to open your mind to some of the specific actions that might be evoked. **You must not predetermine all your responses; that would drain the scene of interaction and spontaneity.** After all, you couldn't possibly know exactly how you would respond to the other character's action since you can't predict what that action will be. Make two or three choices for each line. Send a clear message to your unconscious that these choices are possibilities rather than obligations. Most of all, this work will focus your attention on action and away from emotion. The exercise is particularly useful if you have been receiving criticism for "acting alone," or "indulging in your emotions."

Make Your Choices Specific

When scoring the scene, make your choices specific, physical and colorful. Find choices that excite you, motivate you, and get you more interested in what is happening to you, the character, than what is happening to you, the actor. Try verbs such as *pinch, tickle, corner, caress, test, torment, bait, pacify, lift, tempt, suffocate, guide, titillate,* etc. Experiment with action-filled images: nail him to the wall, run her around in circles, grab him by the shoulders and shake him. Try: shower her with rose petals, pull her hair out, or cover him with kisses. Try: reach over the edge of the precipice and pull her back to safety, take him by the hand and lead him to the path. Experiment with the verbs, then the images, and a combination of the two. Whatever works is right for you, as long as your choices anchor you in the action.

Use With Caution!

Although scoring scenes is a useful strategy, it is a far from foolproof and, if misused, it will backfire. If an obsession with playing your list of marvelous verbs makes you oblivious to what the other characters are doing to you, there will be no interaction. If you fill your mind with events that you anticipate, there will be no room for the events that do occur. Actors who attempt to play action, while eliminating *re*action, may produce a great deal of superficial intensity, yet when all is said and done nothing happens to anyone. The purpose of scoring is to awaken your mind to *possibilities*, thus stimulating your unconscious to make moment-to-moment choices of action. Those final choices, made during the scene—while you are in your character-mind, may seem completely unrelated to your exploration. The probing, however, directed your mind to what happens in the scene: to the *doing*. When the scene begins, dive into the action, freeing yourself of all actor-expectations so you are able to see and hear what is happening. Then you will be free to respond. Please promise me you won't use this exercise to plot out every move of the piece, then, in essence, hand the audience a photocopy of your homework.

Make A Choice Which Gets The Action Into Your Body

If your choices regarding actions are purely intellectual decisions, they are useless to you. Only when the choices are *in your body,* will you be compelled to do. You may be able to get the action into your body if you give the character the opportunity to indulge in fantasy—just as we do in real life. When you fantasize as the character in the contract scene, do you see yourself throwing your brother to the floor, restraining him, then forcing him to sign his name? Find images for your behavior that are vivid, physical, and compelling. Experiment with energy-filled images such as: rake him over the coals; dangle the carrot in front of his nose; build him a castle in the clouds; or drive him out in the open.

Your mental pictures need not always be as obviously dramatic as "raking him over the coals." Not every moment of a script is meant to play at such a fever-pitch. For another scene, your images might include tickling your brother with a feather, or playing a friendly game of chess with him. In a moment filled with sibling affection, you might see yourself pushing him in a backyard swing or building sand castles with him.

Finding a metaphor for the action in the scene may be the secret to fully engaging your mind and body. For example, the contract scene could be a courting dance which might trigger mental images of a male bird strutting and displaying, showing alternating force and passion. In this case, you might attempt to seduce your brother with flattery and you would clearly display your strength. If, on the other hand, you see the scene as a cat-and-mouse affair, your mind will conjure up images of stealth and quiet power. You are more likely to *stalk* your brother, set traps for him and watch intently as he gets within striking distance. The point of finding the metaphor is to discover the poetic reality of a scene, then allow those images to feed your imagination, finally producing a highly individualized literal reality.

When the character's needs permeate your mind and body, you will automatically engage in character action. When you surrender to the character's mission, the character springs to life.

Testing Your Answers

Many actors find identifying action a confusing task. There are so many possibilities and how does one know which ones are best? Don't be discouraged. Don't get bogged down by the need to find the *right* answers—there are none. While some choices serve the script better than others, there are no perfect answers. The point is that by identifying your character's intention or objective, as well as the stakes, and the obstacles, you will plug into the dramatic action. That connection is certain to profoundly affect the playing of the scene. The examination of possibilities will: (1) involve you in the character's thoughts and (2) provide you with something specific upon which you can focus your attention. You are more likely to get in trouble by making no choices than by making the wrong choices. Even if you make choices then later discard them, you are at least focused on character-business. If you can't determine any choices, you probably are consumed by your actor-need for the perfect answer. That overpowering need for the one-and-only answer will create an anxiety that, in turn, produces creative paralysis.

Since some intentions are going to provide a stronger springboard than others, test your choices before you commit. Ask yourself these questions:

1. **Are all your answers stated in first person?**
   Remember that referring to your character in third person ("He or she needs him to sign the contract.") will produce emotional distance between yourself and the character. Create instant connection with the character's needs by stating your questions and answers in first person ("*I* need him to sign the contract.")

2. **Do you experience the needs in your body?**
   Your purpose in answering the questions is to produce a sensation of unrest; you are not preparing to write an essay. For your final check, instead of testing your intellect to see if your choices are valid, scan your body for responses.

3. **Are the stakes high enough?**
   As the actor, you almost always feel you are playing in the Superbowl. Balance the scales by placing the character in a position to have a great deal riding on the outcome of each event. The stakes must be high enough to hold your attention and motivate you to *do*. Only then will the audience see a character in action.

4. **Have you overlooked any obstacles?**
   Have you committed yourself to discovering, then overcoming, every possible obstacle that stands between you and what you want in the scene? Life is full of complications. Don't place your character on a smooth and uninteresting path.

5. **Can you describe your actions with active verbs?**
   Be sure you can describe what you are doing with verbs that take objects, rather than intransitive ones. Choose verbs that will create interaction.

6. **Have you eliminated the conflict?**
   Do your choices clarify the conflicts in your scenes, or have you smoothed out the differences between you and the other characters by putting everyone "on the same team"? Beware of the second kind of choice. If everybody sits around agreeing with each other, where is the action? Where is the "acting in opposition as against a force"? For goodness sake, don't be tempted to turn every scene into a screaming fight because of this mandate to find conflict in your scenes. The give and take is what is essential.

7. **Have you pictured the worst possible scenario?**
   When you consider, in your character-mind, the consequences of failing, you are behaving as people do in real life. We are mobilized not only by our dreams, but by our

nightmares as well. Therefore, you should have, in your character-mind, a vivid picture of what you are trying to prevent. Remember what you (the character) were dreaming about last night when you woke up in a cold sweat. Sometimes you get a clear picture of what you want by focusing on what you are trying to avoid.

8. **Do your choices make you uncomfortable?**

    Your choices should make you feel dissatisfied, vulnerable, uncomfortable, or maybe even a little frightened. If you have finished your preparation and you feel you have settled matters, you no longer care, or you just want to get away from him or her, you have made non-productive choices.

9. **Are your choices stated as simply and briefly as possible?**

    Keep your answers to the point. A few well-chosen images are worth more than endless paragraphs of intellectualizing.

First Aid

If you have racked your brain and still you are no nearer to determining your intention than when you began, try one of the following *Band-Aid* objectives for your first read-through. They will provide some emotional involvement with the other character, and give you some sense of purpose. Besides, while you are busy playing one of these intentions you may intuitively discover the specific action of the scene.

I'm Right and You're Wrong

Your intention is to change the other person's mind. Play "I'm right and you're wrong, and when I can change your mind and get you to agree with me, we will be able to work this out." Commit all your energy to the struggle. Try your best to solve your problem. Note that the formula presupposes you care ("…we will be able to work this out.")

Don't omit any parts of this prescription. Frequently an actor falls into playing what I call, "I'm right and you're wrong, jerk!" The actor rails and rants at the other person, nevertheless nothing happens. The actor in this trap isn't trying to solve a problem—he has assumed the role of reporter and is merely describing unpleasant conditions. That is deadly boring business because the reporter is not attempting to accomplish anything; therefore, there is no action.

Getting To Know You

Boy-gets-girl stories, in particular, will have a "Getting To Know You" scene. In any scene where two people meet for the first time the action revolves around discovery. (See Chapter 9.) These scenes work when the characters encounter every revelation, then each tries to top the other with new disclosures. For example: "You grew up in New York? I did too." "No! Where?" "East 52nd Street." "No kidding. I grew up on East 58th Street."

I've Got A Secret

If you are the investigator in the "I've Got A Secret" scene, you obviously are compelled to get the information the other character can supply. If you are being questioned, you are under equal pressure to withhold the information or to divulge it in a particular way. In other words, you might try to throw the investigator off the track or to point the person in the right direction.

Jump-start

When you can't get a handle on the scene, at least acknowledge that there must be something present that will motivate you to *do*. Even if you can't identify the *psychic itch*, it must exist. If you feel lost, try this jump-start need to keep you focused on problem-solving and pointed toward action. "I don't know why I am dissatisfied, but I am. I also know that the other character in this scene is involved. Furthermore, I won't rest until I have done whatever it takes to fix what's wrong."

In Chapter 14, "Playing The Action," we will elaborate on the subject of *doing*. We have focused, here, on understanding action and discovering what happens in a piece. I hope you see that the concepts in this chapter form the core of this approach to your craft. This notion of *doing* is meant to change your way of looking at the work. It can free you from *paralysis by analysis*. When you focus on action, you free yourself forever from the need to make the lines work. Words are, after all, tools. They are the screwdrivers, hammers, paint-brushes, knives, spoons, wheelbarrows, needles, and pulleys that help your character take care of the doing. The words are not masters you must serve; they are implements that help you accomplish an action. If you play the action, you will be behaving like a real person.

Don't be confused if sometimes you come to an understanding of the action through script analysis, while other times you play the action before you have a firm intellectual grasp of all the elements. The understanding may exist only on an unconscious level. Normally you will discover the action through a combination of analysis and intuition. If you play your part effectively, it doesn't matter whether your perception is conscious or unconscious. You will have a tremendous advantage, however, if you know how to analyze a scene and discover the action in case intuition fails you.

Your preparation should stimulate the unconscious, not become a series of instructions or obligations. Use the questions to awaken your imagination to possibilities. When you have answered the questions and tested your choices, let your unconscious handle this information and commit all your energy to the action between yourself and the other characters. Honestly direct your energy to the tasks that will solve your character's problems. Don't become mired in your analysis of the script and don't monitor your acting. Your discoveries aren't meant to become psychological handcuffs.

The audience watches to see how the action unfolds. While they may be interested in how the characters feel or what they say, they watch primarily to see what the characters in the piece do. They want to see what happens next. The fact is—although it matters to no one how you get there—you must eventually play the action of the scene if you are going to tell the story.

FOOTNOTES

[1]Anita Jesse, *The Playing Is The Thing*, pp. 51-70.

Oft expectation fails and most oft there
Where most it promises.
William Shakespeare,
All's Well that Ends Well,
Act II, Scene 1, Line 145

I was struck all of a heap.
Richard Brinsley Sheridan,
The Duenna Act I, sc. 2

CHAPTER 9

IDENTIFYING THE REVELATIONS

Surprise! Surprise!

Some of the most crucial decisions you make while exploring the script are those that involve what your character knows when the scene begins. If the characters in the piece reveal and discover information, rather than simply re-hashing old material, they will constantly re-align their physical and mental energies to deal with those revelations. Those adjustments provide much of the life force in a scene. A scene without revelations is a scene without surprises for the characters and that scene is long and dull for the characters and the audience. When highway engineers learned that flat, straight highways tend to put drivers to sleep, they began adding a few curves here and there to help keep drivers awake, thereby cutting down on accidents. Characters who don't experience any discoveries, who anticipate all the events in the scene, tend to put audiences to sleep.

THE CHARACTER'S POINT OF INNOCENCE

When playing the scene, always begin from the character's point of innocence. You shouldn't *know* any more than your character *knows*. When a director suggests that you are playing the end of the scene at the beginning, you have failed to correctly establish your character's point of innocence. In your character-mind, don't anticipate anything you will learn during the action. Walk into an emotional ambush. For example, let's say you are playing the younger sibling who tries to persuade the older brother to sign a business contract. (If you need to refresh your memory of the contract scene, refer to "Find The *Psychic Itch*" in Chapter 8.) Compare two choices you might consider during your preparation:

- "I despise him for this. I want to tell him he is deliberately ruining my chance for success."
- "Whatever it takes—come hell or high water—I will get him to sign this contract."

Initially, the first choice may sound productive. It arouses you and, after all, you know that your brother doesn't sign the contract. An actor committed to this choice will defend the decision by citing lines early in the scene in which the brother clearly says he doesn't think it's wise to do business with such a shady guy. The problem with this choice is it places the struggle *offstage*. It means the battle was fought another time, in another place. Since the struggle is precisely what we wanted to see, we will be disappointed. If I reveal the final score for a basketball game you videotaped during the playoffs, you probably will be furious. You wanted to enjoy the contest, with all its surprises and suspense. Similarly, your audience will lose interest in watching you if you play over and over, like a broken record, your disappointment and resentment. If you forecast the end of the scene you are playing, the audience's attention will drift elsewhere, but what is more important, so will yours. Because you are not struggling to overcome the character's obstacles, you risk playing attitudes such as hostility and superiority. Worse still, you will transfer your energy to actor-efforts, since the character's struggles have been minimized and no longer hold your attention.

Look again at the second choice. In this case, each time your brother raises an objection you confront it. Because you, the character, don't know the outcome of the struggle, you fight to win. Now there is an opportunity for action, for something to happen, for surprises. Now your audience will follow your actions and *stay tuned* to see what happens next. The outcome of the scene should be a revelation to all of us—the characters and the audience.

Turning Points

Even minor discoveries in a scene provide subtlety and texture. As the action moves headlong in one direction, revelations alter a character's outlook and the altered perspective produces corrective actions. When confronted with new information, you respond by changing your tactics—you may even change your mind about *what* you want. If you remain oblivious to new information, nothing will happen to you during that moment and the scene will continue in a straight, flat line.

Let's identify some potential revelations in this sample scene:

Walter sits in the back corner booth of the restaurant.
Regina approaches the booth and sits opposite Walter.

Walter
Where is she? I thought she was coming with you.

Regina
(picking up the menu)

Walter
She's not coming, is she?

Regina
No.

Walter
Does she think I had anything to do with this?

Regina
Her lawyer has advised her not to talk to you.

Walter
Her lawyer?
(reaching across the table to grab Regina's arm)
She knows good and well I didn't have anything to do with it.

The first disclosure in this scene is in Regina's failure to respond to: "I thought she was coming with you." The silence indicates the other person is not coming. The later line, "No," is only a verification of what Walter already has surmised. If you are playing Walter, you can inject life into this moment by making the information a discovery. If you decide that you "knew all along she wouldn't show up" you flatten the moment.

The next two lines offer the possibility of another discovery for Walter.

Walter
Does she think I had anything to do with this?

Regina
Her lawyer has advised her not to talk to you.

If you are playing Walter, you could choose to know or suspect that the off-stage character plans to sue you, divorce you or press charges. That choice, however, would lessen the impact of Regina's line. Suppose, instead, that you make the discovery part of your action. During the interchange you learn that this person has hired a lawyer. That adjustment forces you to take in the revelation, then re-align your mental and physical energy to cope with the potential crisis. The latter choice is more dynamic and presents a greater potential for involving you, as well as your audience, in the action.

Characters don't always verbalize their messages. Sometimes they reveal the information, either deliberately or unintentionally, with body language, facial expressions, or tone of voice. For example, if Walter roughly grabs Regina's arm, Regina gets a sense of Walter's current emotional state. As Regina, you could vitalize this moment by deliberately underestimating Walter's desperation. Now, his action may surprise you and the audience will feel your adjustment to the new information. Of course some physical actions, such as this one, might not be indicated in the script. They may be revealed only when you are on your feet with the scene.

Your revelations will include the information you learn about the other characters in the scene, the people referred to in the conversation, and yourself. In the scene above, Regina may have to adjust to Walter's unexpected mental state, while Walter must face the betrayal by an off-stage character. As Walter, you could also treat the moment when you roughly grab Regina's arm as a revelation. (If you thought you had your emotions under control, your loss of composure may upset you.)

Make Dangerous Choices

A scene that isn't working may be off-track simply because one of the actors has explained away a potentially painful discovery. In our example, the actor playing Walter may have reasoned: "Oh, I decided that I knew all along she would think I was guilty. It doesn't surprise me a bit that she has hired a lawyer. This is typical." If you habitually eliminate revelations in this manner, you are insulating yourself emotionally. You are maneuvering to avoid the shock, then pain, that would come from facing the betrayal. Your recognition of the treachery, and the resulting adjustment may be vital parts of the action in the scene. Naturally your actor-self will want to avoid the possibility of facing betrayal—it's not a pleasant experience.

If you haven't learned to open yourself up to all your emotions, you will unconsciously maneuver to protect yourself from pain and confusion. Part of your job as an actor is learning to thwart your own basic survival instincts. In other words, you learn to set yourself up for the very misfortunes you try to avoid in real life. You deliberately walk into those emotional ambushes.

Make your revelations potent by endowing them with genuine significance. Avoid choices that leave you apathetic. Make choices that are emotionally dangerous—choices that set you up to be humiliated, frightened, enraged, disgusted, swept away by joy or love.

Expect The Opposite

After you have identified the revelations and made choices filled with emotional danger, prepare yourself to play the moments of discovery truthfully. You cannot act out a discovery any more than you can play a feeling or play your given circumstances. If you do try to play the revelation, you will have to *act* shocked, disgusted, afraid, etc. **To truthfully play the moment as a revelation, you must identify what you learn during the action, then set up in your character-mind an expectation of the opposite.** Take for example, the moment when you hear: "Her lawyer has advised her not to talk to you." The announcement will surprise you only if you have been thinking: "I know she's upset but when I explain what happened she will come around." Only if you expect her to be on your side—and later learn that she won't be—does this become a moment of discovery and a turning point in the action.

Don't Overdo It

Sometimes I think that every tool I talk about should be labeled with a caution sign: "WARNING: May be hazardous to your work." If you manipulated every moment of a scene into one revelation after another, you would turn your character into an idiot. Allow the revelations to provide turning points. On the other hand, keep in mind that, like any other aspect of your script exploration, balance is essential.

Make room for your character's discoveries. Ignoring or denying revelations is a way of eliminating the obstacles in a character's path. **When you eliminate obstacles in a scene you create a smooth, uninteresting road for your character and smooth, uninteresting viewing for the audience.**

A pilot who sees from afar will not make his boat a wreck.
Amen-em-apt, *Teaching How To Live*

CHAPTER 10

CHECKLIST

Prepare For Take-Off

When you have determined your character's given circumstances and identified the action and the discoveries made during each scene, run through this checklist. Use the following questions to discover whether or not you have overlooked anything. Test your answers to be certain that you have made productive choices. While you can never hope to attain perfection in your work, you can avoid common pitfalls.

1. **Have you defined your character's given circumstances?**
   Bring your character's world to life by establishing details that are specific and vivid. This imaginary context is where you must *live*. (Did you answer all the questions in Chapter 7?)

2. **Do you know what you need?**
   Have you clearly defined your needs applying the guidelines in Chapter 8? Have you subjected your choices to the test at the end of that chapter?

3. **Have you identified the revelations?**
   Have you furnished your character surprises and provided turning points in the action?

4. **Have you done all your exploration in the first person?**
   Answer all the questions in the first person, never the third person. Don't talk about the character from a safe, objective point of view. These are *your* problems, *your* needs, not *hers* or *his*.

5. **Are your choices emotionally colorful?**
   Your choices must have emotional clout and must be stated in human feeling terms. The purpose of the exploration is to stimulate your unconscious into life. Don't expect dry, lifeless lists to awaken the creator within you.

6. Have you judged the character?

To illuminate the character you must be willing to get inside the character's mind and concern yourself with his or her goals and struggles. Even the most reprehensible criminal believes his actions are totally justifiable. Selfish people will defend their behavior as appropriately prudent. Greedy people believe they deserve a larger share because of greater need or because they have earned more. Arrogant people view themselves as inarguably superior; and so on. Don't allow analyzing, judging, and labeling to create a gulf between you and the character. Distance from your character is the last thing you want. The goal of preparation is to bring you and the character together.

7. Have you judged the material?

Take a look at what the piece asks of you. Are you unwilling to go through what the character must experience? Have you judged the character? Have you ignored or denied the character's revelations? Make an effort to uncover the life in the piece. If you are correct and the writing is mediocre (or worse), all the judging in the world won't make your preparation or playing any easier. If you can't commit to the material, you should turn down the job.

8. Have you remained flexible?

Treat the discoveries that result from your exploration of given circumstances, action, and revelations as possibilities. As the work progresses, your initial discoveries will be tempered. Further study of the script, *aha's* that can occur only in the playing, and contributions from the director will add texture to your original discoveries. Regard every choice as a springboard, never a straitjacket.

If you are off-course, referring to this checklist can help put you on the right path. But, make no mistake about it, reading this checklist once won't change your work habits. Ask yourself these questions after each preparation until you are consistently avoiding all the common pitfalls.

I have always thought the actions of men the best inter-
preters of their thoughts.

John Locke,
An Essay Concerning Human Understanding

CHAPTER 11

CREATING A CHARACTER

Actor + Action = Character

Characterization emerges when you play the action truthfully. When you (1) immerse yourself in the character's given circumstances, (2) surrender to the character's needs, and (3) commit to playing the character's action, you reveal the character. In truth, if you do these things it will be impossible to conceal the character.

CHARACTER IS REVEALED BY DOING

When some actors use the term "characterization," they are talking about externals
such as body language, facial tics, physical disabilities, dialect, etc. However, those externals tell us little about who the character is. Characterization is the human being revealed
by the doing.

HOLD THE MIRROR UP TO NATURE

In real life, you make decisions about who people are by observing what they do.
How many times have you met someone, formed a first impression, then later reevaluated
the person based on actions? No matter how unimpressed you were with a person origi-

nally, you formed a new opinion if deeds warranted. If later that person returned your wallet, spoke up for you in a touchy situation, or saved a friend from embarrassment, you formed a new image in your mind. The doing provided more significant data than the externals that contributed to your first impression. How many times have you been disappointed by someone who had "talked a good game"? Perhaps the person made glowing promises or at least implied that he or she was dependable. You may have been charmed and impressed by this individual's air of confidence and pledges of loyalty or dedication. Later, however, when the person didn't deliver the work, or broke the trust, you made a new assessment based on the more important evidence of doing.

Keep in mind these simple and common life-lessons when you begin character work. The character will be revealed by the doing. While you may find it fascinating to give your character a limp, a lisp, a facial tic, or an accent, those of us in the audience don't care about those externals *unless* they are accompanied by actions. If you fall in love with externals, you may concentrate on your limp rather than providing your character an inner life. You are likely to be so distracted by your eagerness to show the limp that you fail to play the action. Consequently, your performance leaves us with vivid images of your gait, and perhaps we are impressed by your accurate representation of the physical condition. But your rendering of the character will not genuinely touch us, because the shortage of character-action robbed us of the character's story.

Thorough Preparation Will Set You Free

To make sure your character has depth, reality and resonance, rather than slick externals, dig into the script. Begin by reading and re-reading the script until it penetrates your consciousness. Your goal is to assimilate the material, in much the same way you absorb food. Soon after you eat a meal, there comes a moment when there is no longer a point where the substance you consumed stops and you begin. You have digested the food and it becomes a part of your cells. The food is not *in* you; the food *is* you. Your goal is to digest the script—you want to read and re-read it until it is a part of you. (See Chapter 7, "Defining The Given Circumstances" for specifics.)

Daydream every detail and nuance of the character's context into existence. Get into the character's skin and discover what you crave, what it will take to make you happy, what motivates you. Lend the character your mind, body and heart for the fulfillment of these needs. (Turn to Chapter 8, "Discovering The Dramatic Action," if you need to review character needs.)

Each conclusion you reach during script exploration contributes to the molding of the character you will portray. When you define the given circumstances, you specify the context that shapes the character's personality and you set in motion the impetus for particular needs and wants. Those needs, in turn, will evoke actions and the particular actions will reveal the individuality. Notice that you, and all the people around you, exemplify these principles. Your upbringing provided a network of experiences that instilled certain values, provided particular skills, contributed to your point of view, and shaped your personality. Your circumstances spark needs, and what you do to fulfill those needs exposes who you are.

Qualities Should Provide Clues To Behavior

In addition to searching the script for the given circumstances and dramatic action, inspect the dialogue for clues related to your character's personality. Digest what other characters say about you and what you say about them. For example, in Act II of *A Doll's House* Krogstad calls Nora "a sensitive, petted creature."[1] Earlier in the same scene, Nora tells Krogstad to "be good enough to speak respectfully of my husband."[2] If you are playing Nora, these lines are valuable clues to your character—weigh the information supplied by the two against one another. What actions do they suggest?

During your examination of the dialogue you may compile a list of adjectives describing your character. While I wouldn't tell you to avoid this technique, I will warn you that such adjectives are virtually meaningless unless you connect them to action. Descriptions such as *shy, gentle,* and *intelligent* can be useful information so long as you remember they are nothing more than hints. **You can play the actions suggested by qualities, but you can't play the qualities themselves.** Follow up on the clues, using your dictionary. You will discover that the definitions for the adjectives you have selected frequently include either a specific, or at least implied, reference to actions. For instance, one of the definitions for *shy* is *retiring.* Pursuing the clue further, you would discover that *The American College Dictionary,* for example, defines *retire* as a verb meaning "to withdraw, or go away or apart." *Retiring* is defined as "withdrawing from contact with others." These are actions you can play. Trying to play a quality, without incorporating action, most often leads actors to play stereotypes, or affect attitudes. An actor playing *shy* doesn't accurately portray a shy person. While the misguided actor will try to create an impression of shyness, that is exactly what a shy person tries to avoid. A truly shy person aches to appear confident and comfortable, therefore, would never *act* shy.

Play The Character, Not The Therapist

Again, I urge you to work in first person while probing for information about your character. Repeat these two statements aloud and notice what happens to you:

- From outside the character: "My character is a bitch."
- From inside the character: "The bastard owes me more than half. I worked like a dog to help him get everything he has."

Obviously the second choice creates involvement with the character's needs, while the first answer, useless name-calling and pseudo-analysis, will deepen the chasm that separates you from the character. The first choice leaves you free to observe from a safe distance, the second one is apt to *get under your skin* and evoke action. Bear in mind, you want to play the character, not the character's therapist. The therapist is concerned with analysis; you are looking for actions to play.

Learn To Work Fast

Although extensive script exploration is invaluable for discovering your character, in some cases—particularly if you work in TV—you may have very little time for preparation. In those instances, you will play characters close to yourself or characters you have previously developed. Keep in mind that it isn't uncommon to audition for episodic TV on Thursday and shoot on Friday. Such a hectic schedule leaves little time for script examination. More than likely you will get the job only if the producers want you to play one of the "everyday *you's*," or if they want to see aspects of yourself you have discovered in another preparation period.

Use Every Trick In The Book

Allow props and costumes to stimulate your unconscious. Cinderella's fairy godmother knew what she was doing when she gave her protégé those slippers. Your shoes influence your gait, of course, and at the same time they bring out different you's. If you don't wear your sloppiest old sneakers to a dress-up affair, it's partly because you don't want to attend the special occasion as the you who wears those old beat-up shoes. You may prefer to enjoy the affair as the dress-up you. Because you know that your shoes will influence the way you stand, walk, and even how you sit, you may choose whichever shoes evoke the you that you want to take to the ball. Everything you wear or carry has a similar impact. Explore all the possibilities available to you with costumes and props.

Review all the chapters in this book for exercises that may free you to discover the character's given circumstances, needs and actions. For example, use "Go Inside The Picture," from Chapter 2, to help you bring your character's context into focus. While you are *inside the picture,* open your mind. Welcome the character's psychic itch and fantasize the actions that might satisfy those needs.

THERE ARE MORE THAN ENOUGH YOU'S TO FILL THE CHARACTER

Most actors in my workshops welcome this straightforward approach I have described for creating character. They learn quickly that they can depend upon circumstances, needs, and actions to help them breathe life into a character. On the other hand, I occasionally encounter actors who find this method too simple to trust. The lack of confidence stems, I believe, from a desire to make the job more cerebral. Some actors seem disappointed to learn that they can't substitute analysis of the character for playing the action. After all, analysis provides a safe, sterile space, while getting inside the character's skin requires a kind of abandonment that can get messy.

More often, however, actors who don't trust this process are, in truth, dealing with fear—fear they won't be enough. They fear that they need to be more than they are to play the role effectively—that they need to create a brand new, unfamiliar *someone,* then imitate that person. Nothing could be further from the truth. For one thing, you are already different *you's* in varying circumstances, depending on the real-life roles you are playing. You may have been playing these roles so long you are no longer conscious of the adjustments required to sustain the effect; nonetheless, they exists. The person you are when you are in your parents' home for Christmas is quite different from the person you are in a restaurant on a date. The *you* who works comfortably at your desk is unlike the *you* on the freeway who feels hassled by traffic. In real life, we all respond to our given circumstances and various facets of our psychological make-up dominate as our situation changes.

Make Your Entire Self Available

You might find it useful to think of characterization as allowing the character to pick and choose from your psyche whatever aspects of you are needed. Some actors think of characterization as getting the everyday *you* out of the way, thus making room for the character to fill you up. You accomplish either of these objectives by:

- committing to the character's given circumstances
- surrendering to the character's needs
- executing the character's actions

You trust that your commitment to your choices and your belief in the given circumstances will direct your unconscious to tap into the *you* that will fill this role. You are, after all, much more than the ego-self you present to the world. Even your most intimate family and friends see only a slightly expanded version of that ego-self. Your ego-self is the aggregate of personal and social traits you have been organizing and re-organizing all your life. It is the temperament, or disposition, you have as a result of genetics and life experiences.

The personality you present to the world reflects your selection of a particular range of behaviors over all others. You discovered that comfortable range through countless instances of trial and error in which you struggled for emotional, perhaps even physical, survival. If you believe that staying within that range of behaviors has kept you alive, it is no wonder that you can't imagine yourself functioning outside your carefully erected boundaries. You may be convinced that you are only the *you* that is bounded by the limits of your ego-self. For instance, because, thus far, you have believed it advantageous to suppress any impulse to demonstrate your toughness, you may think that there is no toughness in you. In truth, the potential still exists for you to express all the *you's* deep inside that you have never before realized.

Allow Your Unconscious To Surprise You

Like a great body of water, a human being is much more than its outward appearance. When we look at a lake, we see, at first glance, a flat surface, nonetheless we know that the illusion is misleading. We know that the surface is constantly in motion, even if the movement is barely visible, and that beneath the surface are deep pools, hidden currents and murky shallows. Bring your whole self to your work—all the currents, pools, and shallows. It doesn't matter that you don't know, with your conscious mind, about all those potentialities.

Place yourself in an environment that you can—through your imagination—see, hear, taste, touch and smell. Deal with people whom you also perceive with all your sense organs and with whom you have very specific relationships. Have a reason to be in this place at this time, and accept the imaginary circumstances as your personal reality. Allow the needs of the character to push aside your own needs. Experience all the mental and physical action as though these things were happening not to someone else, not to an imaginary person, but to you. Now you can expect your unconscious to call up the behavior that is appropriate, or the *you* that is suitable.

Give your character unlimited freedom to roam the depths of your psyche. Hold nothing back for the sake of ego. Have the courage to give your character *the run of the castle*. Be certain there are no secret passages and no locked diaries. Be brave. Allow the character to dredge up aspects of your being you long-ago buried. Permit the character to outrage, delight, torment, terrify and sanctify you with these forgotten shards of your self. Remember that the sort of acting to which the artist aspires is a process of revealing the inner soul. If you trust the work, you can tap into hidden aspects of yourself through the magic flight provided by imagination and the solid guidance guaranteed by preparation and concentration.

FOOTNOTES

[1]Henrik Ibsen, *A Doll's House*, trans. Michael Meyer (Garden City, NY: Anchor Books, Doubleday and Company, Inc., 1966) Act II, p. 70.
[2]Ibsen, p. 69.

So she went into the garden to cut a cabbage leaf to make an apple pie; and at the same time a great she-bear, coming up the street, pops its head into the shop. 'What! no soap?' So he died, and she very imprudently married the barber; and there were present the Picninnies, and the Joblillies, and the Baryulies, and the Grand Panjandrum himself, ... and they all fell to playing the game of catch as catch can, till the gunpowder ran out at the heels of their boots.

Samuel Foote,
Nonsense written to test the boasted memory
of Charles Macklin, *The Quarterly Review*

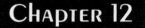

CHAPTER 12

LEARNING THE LINES

Making A Sticky Surface

If you have trouble remembering your lines on-stage, you need to investigate your mechanics of storing and retrieving information so you can discover exactly where the breakdown occurs. You may be storing information ineffectively. Perhaps you are burying it amid a pile of psychic clutter, making it almost impossible to find. On the other hand, you may be adept at storage, then fail at the retrieval process. Perhaps you are too distracted during performance to access what you mentally filed. Let's look, first, at some techniques for helping you more effectively store the dialogue in your mind.

CREATE A TEXTURED SURFACE TO
WHICH THE WORDS WILL ADHERE

Don't separate learning dialogue from the rest of the preparation process. Learn the lines the way you learned the words to your favorite song, or the way you learned nursery rhymes when you were a child. That wasn't drudgery. You learned the words because they interested you. Involve yourself in the script exploration in a way that causes you to absorb the lines or assimilate them. Avoid rote memorization, as in memorizing the multiplication tables. While preparing, concentrate exclusively on the script; maintain intense curiosity; and commit to a deep emotional involvement. If you follow those guidelines, you will begin to learn the lines from the very first reading. As you digest the script and get inside the skin of the character, you will discover that you are learning most of the words effortlessly. As you probe the script and make choices, you create an intricate design of mental images and this design functions as a textured surface to which the words will adhere.

Find The Trigger

Each of your lines has a *trigger*. Something that is said or done ignites a reaction, you formulate a thought, then finally express something in response to your thought. Once you find the triggers, your lines are no longer words you struggle to cram into your memory. You transform them into essential tools, then you will eagerly reach for them to express the thoughts that burn in your mind. That trigger may occur in the line immediately before yours or in a speech given minutes before yours. In some cases, you may never find anything in the script that obviously explains why you say what you do. (I have included an example of such a line later in this section.)

Often the trigger is apparent. For example, let's say the line before yours is, "I only wanted to protect you." Your line is: "Seems like the only thing I need protection from is you." Since you repeat the root word *protect*, that is clearly the word that fires the thought you express. Because you are making the point that this person has not only failed to protect you but has actually harmed you, support that position with detailed *remember when's*. Relive in your imagination—supplying vivid details—the occasions when you needed protection while this person, instead, betrayed and deceived you. Now you won't have to *memorize* the line. When you hear the words "I only wanted to protect you," memories of treachery will flood your mind, and your emotional response will almost certainly trigger your line.

Sometimes when words or actions trigger a thought, you suppress the impulse to respond. Perhaps you *stew* over a comment and *nurse* hurt feelings, or maybe you are merely distracted for a time and *shelve* a thought for later. For this type of trigger, you may have to go back several speeches to find the stimulus. Another type of trigger is one where the words and actions in one speech by another character triggers several of your speeches. Look for instances where you appear to hear little of what anyone else says for a time, continuing, instead, on one train of thought while someone else attempts to get your attention.

Some lines seem to come from out of nowhere. In Horton Foote's *The Roads to Home, (A Nightingale)* Vonnie, has a number of lines in that category. For example:

> **Mabel.** Wet years, you know, are death on the cotton. My Papa used to always say, 'I don't care how dry it gets, we'll always make some kind of a crop, but when it starts in raining you can just forget cotton and everything else.'
>
> **Vonnie.** Annie, what church are you affiliated with?[1]

Imagine you are playing Vonnie. No one has mentioned religion so far, yet, obviously, something makes you think of church. Find that stimulus. Maybe it's the image of dark skies and rainy days that is triggered by Mabel's speech. Perhaps you recall a period when you were a child. The rain fell for days on end and you remember your mother crying softly and your father assuring her that "Even if the cotton crop fails, we'll survive somehow. The good Lord will take care of us." Connect that to pictures of your family in church, praying for help "in these difficult times." Now when Mabel begins to talk about "wet years," those images will come to your mind along with your line.

I have noticed that the actors in my classes become quite adept at learning lines quickly once they grasp this concept of triggers. When you identify the pattern that links the thoughts, you change your relationship to the words. Instead of foreign matter that you feel obligated to shove into your brain, the words become a means to an end. You need them to express the thoughts that are being evoked. Identifying triggers is a little like lining up dominoes so that when you tip one over, it knocks over the next; and so on. So long as you don't leave too much space between the dominoes, tipping over the first one sets off a chain reaction. As a result of your preparation, you don't have to knock over each domino, one at a time. It is the careful arrangement of the objects in the preparation stage that produces the effect, rather than a continuous manual effort. (For a more detailed discussion of triggers, see "Finding The Triggers" in *The Playing Is The Thing*.)[2]

Use Imagery

When your dialogue includes narration, be certain to image what you describe. *See* the pictures in your mind's eye; *hear* the sounds in your mind's ear; delight in the familiar odors. *Relive* the moment you will depict, using all your senses. Now you are not memorizing words; you are imprinting your mind with images. When you come to that moment in the scene, *recall* the event you want to share and, with relatively little study, you will take possession of the words the character uses to describe the event. For example, another character in *A Nightingale*, Mabel Votaugh, describes Annie Gayle's father:

> [H]e made money every which way he turned. He had a store, he made money. He owned farms, he made money. He had a ranch, he made money. He was a president of the bank. And then we had a series of crop failures and his best friend was a planter named Sledge and Mr. Sledge had seven years of crop failures and he kept borrowing from the bank to keep going and one day Mr. Gayle, that was her father's name, without any warning, Mr. Sledge said, foreclosed on him and took all of his land and his plantation house. And that same afternoon Mr. Sledge came into town as Mr. Gayle came out of the bank with Annie and Mr. Sledge, they say called his

name, and Mr. Gayle walked over to him. He shot him, killing him, right in front of Annie.[3]

Learn this passage by imaging the story. *Cast* someone you know as Mr. Gayle, then picture him literally making money. Watch him cut the paper and print it; there are piles of it everywhere he turns. See the store. Go inside. Examine the specific merchandise, particularly things you desire. Smell the odors in the air. Buy something. Notice Mr. Gayle behind a counter making more money. Visit Mr. Gayle at the farm, the ranch and the bank. Observe the devastated crops in the ravaged fields and the despairing farmers. See Mr. Gayle with his arm on Mr. Sledge's shoulder. Substitute a specific person for Mr. Sledge (putting an enormous sledge hammer in his hand might help you remember his name) and watch him planting row after row of crops. Visualize Mr. Sledge's crop shriveling and dying, then witness his despair. It may help to see giant sevens growing in the fields, then dying. Watch Mr. Sledge repeatedly going to the bank carrying out baskets of money. If you continue in this manner (seeing and hearing the foreclosure, then the murder) until you master all the facts of the story, much of the memorization of lines will happen coincidentally.

Put It In Your Own Words

Put the character's thoughts into your own words. Read a speech, express the thoughts in your own words, then immediately read the speech as written. Repeat this process several times, until you own the character's words. Don't make this technique an excuse to be slovenly about learning the author's dialogue. You may be having trouble with a speech because you do not fully understand it and putting it into your own words will force you to confront the degree of your comprehension. Don't memorize your own words; use them only to bring you closer to the character's words. Especially in the case of highly stylized dialogue, the words can feel like a moat separating you from the character. This technique of making the words yours is like building a bridge to cross that moat.

You can't very well translate your character's thoughts into your phraseology if you don't understand the meanings of the words that constitute your dialogue. If you don't already own a well-used dictionary, run, don't walk, to your nearest bookstore.

Learn The Lines Without Sacrificing Spontaneity

If you memorize your lines by repeating, over and over, set line readings, you will lock yourself into a no-win situation. With this type of preparation, you can either act alone and remember your lines or connect with the other actors and constantly need prompting. Your dilemma isn't produced by a defective memory; it results from a faulty method of storage. By drilling line readings you have intertwined the words with specific emotional content, making it impossible to disentangle them. Anything that eliminates one obliterates the other. Now the only way your lines can be triggered is if the plotted emotion is evoked. An unanticipated emotional response will dislodge the line and leave you with a blank mind. In defense, you stop listening, since the other actor is likely to affect you in a way you failed to anticipate. This faulty storage method is one reason why some actors give cold readings full of life and spontaneity then go deadly flat after learning their lines. These actors have formed the habit of not listening to shelter the lines they so painstakingly memorized.

If you are in the habit of practicing line readings, break up your old patterns. Try saying the lines differently each time. Say them in a sing-song type monotone, go over them while sitting still, repeat them on your feet and moving, sing them—anything to avoid fixed patterns. The logical mind is quick to decide what is right and wrong and loves the refuge of predictability; however, your creative spirit yearns for flexibility.

Preparation Will Pay Off

If you approached this chapter hoping it would focus on shortcuts to learning lines, you may be disappointed. Although the triggers concept does help some actors become fast studies, by and large, these methods require a considerable amount of time and energy. The big payoff comes in increased efficiency. You may end up spending as much time as ever learning lines, but this approach will eliminate much of the struggle and, what's more important, it promises you greater recall. Besides, this technique will guarantee that even if you should forget a few words in performance, you can easily get back on track. The *sticky surface* you have created will keep you oriented in the story.

Acquiring new and improved techniques for learning lines helps. Nevertheless, you still need to practice this skill just as you would practice any other in which you want to excel. Develop the habit of committing to memory some words every day. Learn a poem, a speech by a favorite character, a quotation from a favorite author, phrases from a song—anything that brings you pleasure. Begin by memorizing just a line or two and gradually, as your skill increases, you will easily retain longer passages.

Accessing What You Stored

I wish I could promise you that a competent job of learning your lines would guarantee perfect recall. Unfortunately, there is another consideration. Although you probably will be under only moderate stress when storing the information, you will be under severe pressure when retrieving the information. Your ability to recall what you have learned depends upon not only the efficiency of storage, but the basic skills you have been sharpening. Here is yet another reason to master concentration, listening, and relaxation.

Directors and stage managers often hear the complaint, "I knew these lines at home, now I can't remember any of them." In these situations, accusations may fly; however, the actor is probably telling the truth. In a comfortable situation, the person easily recalled the lines. Indeed, all the words remain safely stored in the actor's memory. The actor *knows* the line but has blocked *access* to the information. You can do a terrific job of storing information, then inhibit the retrieval process. I have seen an actor stumble on every other line during a run-through of a scene then, only moments later, be letter-perfect on dialogue. The difference is concentration and relaxation.

Often, learned lines aren't accessible because they are shut off behind a wall of hysterical *what if's*: "what if I forget my lines?" "what if I don't hear my cue." During performance, does your concentration ever wander from the immediate moment to worry about what is coming up later in the scene? If you are projecting ahead, wondering if you will be able to recall lines that should come up half a page later in the scene, you will certainly miss your triggers. During your preparation, you arranged for a chain reaction of thoughts and actions triggering succeeding thoughts and actions. Leave room in your mind for that sequence of events. Perhaps during performance your worrywart of a self-critic needles you about a line due to come up half a page from now. Think of real-life conversations. Off-stage, you probably don't plan responses now, hoping they will be appropriate two to three minutes later. But you will know what to say when you get there! Stay in the moment by focusing on character-concerns and pay attention to the people around you, assuming that what they say and do will evoke responses from you.

In some instances you have trouble retrieving lines because you have buried them beneath a barrage of self-criticism. The pathway to your mental data bank is piled with debris. Your mental energy will be funneled into supporting your rotten opinion of yourself. Besides, if you are busy indulging in self-flagellation, you won't hear your cues. Clear your mind and listen to those around you rather than to your negative self-talk. Keep the pathway to the information clear.

Ultimately, you must trust your preparation. Have the discipline to learn the words, and the courage to forget them. Regardless of how much time you spend with the script you may find that the critic in you whispers, "Bet you don't know these words!" Once you complete your preparation, trust that you have imbedded the words in your character-mind and properly linked them to your cues. If you continue to have trouble remembering your lines, work on your concentration skills.

FOOTNOTES

[1]Horton Foote, *The Roads To Home* (New York: Dramatists Play Service, Inc., 1982) p. 14. Copyright, Horton Foote, 1982.
[2]Anita Jesse, *The Playing Is The Thing*, pp. 169-178.
[3]Horton Foote, p. 11.

Allowing The Part To Play You

Make Wings, Not Hobbles

We cannot *will* to have insights. We cannot *will* creativity. But we can *will* to give ourselves to the encounter with intensity of dedication and commitment. The deeper aspects of awareness are activated to the extent that the person is committed to the encounter.

Rollo May, *The Courage To Create*

Allowing The Part To Play You

Make Wings, Not Hobbles

By now, it should be apparent to you that your basic skills and your preparation are what will eventually set you free. I hope it is equally clear that, by advising you to allow the part to play you, I'm not recommending carelessness. Allowing the part to play you does not imply that you neglect basic skills, skip preparation, say a prayer to the acting gods and hope for the best. I hope you will want your work to *appear* effortless but, like most endeavors that depend upon execution without strain to be effective, acting requires diligent preparation. To cite another example, the art of the dancer is in making the dance appear effortless, spontaneous and inevitable. We appreciate those qualities; nevertheless we know full well that the dancer has invested many long hours in training and rehearsal.

Similarly, the effective actor causes people to believe that anyone can act—it looks so easy. As a student of the art, you are learning that you need considerable skill to make acting look simple and that it takes time to acquire the skill. First, there is the ongoing work to develop your concentration, imagination, listening and observation skills, and to reclaim your emotions and attain relaxation. You also have discovered that you must invest as much time as possible on the specific groundwork for each role. You probe at and pore over the script until you discover the given circumstances, determine the dramatic action and identify the revelations. You relentlessly pursue this information because you know it will provide you with specific points of concentration and protect you from playing generalities. Ideally, you will have a gestation period during which you can assimilate these facts. All this work just to make acting look easy!

In the following chapters, we will take a look at some techniques that will help you move from the preparatory phase to the performance phase. These techniques will help prepare you for the time when you must release your death grip on all those friendly, reliable facts that you discovered during script exploration. As comforting as those facts may be, ultimately, they are only a springboard for the performance. When it is time to "get on your feet"—it is time to allow the part to play you. You can fulfill that objective only if you are willing to let go of the preparation and free yourself to live in the character's present moments. This letting go takes courage, but, if you lack that courage, you will never succeed in breathing life into your character. Keep in mind that concentrating on your preparation while playing the scene is equivalent to driving while focusing exclusively on your rear-view mirror. Both are dangerous tactics. If your homework fills the center of your awareness, you cannot be conscious of what is happening in the present moment. You are living, instead, in the past and in your actor-past at that. You are twice removed from the character's present moment.

Don't kid yourself that you can concentrate on both your preparation and the character's needs; it is absolutely impossible. I cannot emphasize this point too much. I am a major proponent of preparedness for actors; indeed, I have little patience with those who advise actors that any and all homework interferes with authenticity and spontaneity. On the other hand, I am also convinced that the best acting occurs only when you are willing to release the preparation, stop thinking about it, and *play*, or *do*. Only when you yield to the character's needs can you surprise yourself and tap into what you don't know that you know. You see, the trouble with what you *know* is that it is often a cliché. What you know is comprised of things you've seen before and expect to happen. Leave room for the unexpected.

Never lose sight of the fact that you want to create the illusion that everything you do and feel is spontaneous, requires no actor effort, and is absolutely inevitable. Letting go doesn't mean that you skimp on preparation. Furthermore, it doesn't imply that you should step on-stage blindly trusting that everything is going to work out just because you have done thorough preparation. Letting the part play you means that your acting matches the following description. **You wholeheartedly embrace the character's given circumstances as though they were your own and place your character concerns at the center of your awareness. You devote your physical and mental energies to satisfying the character's needs. You trust yourself to behave spontaneously and truthfully, thus telling the character's story and, in the process, you reveal the character.**

Our life is like some vast lake that is slowly filling with the stream of our years. As the waters creep surely upward the landmarks of the past are one by one submerged. But there shall always be memory to lift its head above the tide until the lake is overflowing.

Alexandre Charles Auguste Bisson, *Madame X*

CHAPTER 13

PLAYING WITHIN THE GIVEN CIRCUMSTANCES

Open The Floodgates Of The Past

By defining your character's given circumstances, as described in Chapter 7, you give him or her a personal history. Vivid and personal choices will provide you with a rich inner life—a mental suitcase of character thoughts. Those thoughts will supply a reason for listening to the people you are talking to and add deeper meaning to their words. Your choices will create a specific reference point for the events and a filter system through which all stimuli must pass before it reaches you. It is nearly impossible to overestimate the significance of the given circumstances. You could play the same character a dozen times; yet, each time you created a new filter system, you would produce profoundly different nuances in the playing.

YOU CANNOT PLAY THE GIVEN CIRCUMSTANCES

The given circumstances provide a container, or arena, in which the events of the scene take place. Don't try to play the container. Certainly, in your day-to-day living, you don't *play* your own personal history. Once you establish your character-world, have the courage to turn your attention away from your preparation and devote yourself to the action. Don't show us your homework. Have confidence that the work you have done will affect your playing of the scene. The context you have defined forms a lens through which you, the character, perceive the actions of others. Trust your perception of events to shape your responses.

PLANTING LAND MINES

Imagine a real-life example of how our circumstances affect us. If someone mentions your mother, you don't search your mind for images of her and struggle to produce an emotional response. The intricate combination of reactions in your mind and body is automatic and beyond your conscious control. Those reactions are connected to a complex relationship of very specific events in your life. You don't will them into existence. At best, you might inhibit some outward manifestations of your response, nevertheless that would be the extent of your control. Your response is, in a sense, a knee-jerk reaction. By defining the given circumstances in your script, you provide your character with knee-jerk reactions. Construct an inner life for your character by supplying memories and allow the action in the scene to spark those memories. I call this process planting land mines. Load your emotional landscape with *remember when's* and you can be certain that when you cross that terrain you will set off some blasts.

USE DAYDREAMING AND *REMEMBERING* TO IMPROVE THE INTERCHANGE

While we are on this subject of daydreaming and *remembering* imaginary events, I must caution you about a related technique: sense memory work. Often actors are advised to focus, during a scene, on emotional memories. The memories are used to call up particular feelings. Even people who have never attended an acting class have heard about recalling your dog's death while you play the scene in which your sister is dying.

Unquestionably, the loss of a beloved pet taught you painful lessons about grief and what you learned can contribute immeasurably to your understanding of a character's circumstances. I still experience sharp stabs of grief when I recall the last few days I had with a beloved Arab gelding I lost almost five years ago. Every time I recount the events leading up to his death I end up crying. If you watched me talk about him, and you couldn't hear the words, you wouldn't know whether I was talking about an animal or a person. The results would be the same if I were talking about my Shetland Sheepdog who died almost *fifteen* years ago. Grief is grief is grief is grief.

Unfortunately, I have seen confused actors who clearly misunderstand the use of emotional memory. I once saw the actor cast as a grieving relative, leave an audience, not only unmoved, but totally confused. During potentially wrenching dialogue, the actor playing the survivor stared into space, all the while stroking the fabric of the sofa on which the *dying* brother lay. When I asked the actor what he was doing, and why he seemed oblivious to his brother, the actor confessed that he was doing his sense memory work. He said he was stroking the fur of the dog who had meant so much to him when he was a child. When the dog died, it had left him devastated and he was trying to recreate that sense of anguish by remembering how it felt to pet the animal.

The actor had chosen an appropriate stimulus—the death of a trusted and adored friend; however, he needed to have confidence in his homework. It might have been very useful to recall the comradeship of the dog and the anguish suffered over his death. Even recreating those sensations by touching the animal's fur may have been valuable, but that should have been covered in the homework phase. When the time comes to play the scene, you must have faith that the wounds you have opened during preparation will be inflamed by the actions of your brother and yourself. The events you have chosen to help you connect with the character's circumstances must not become the focal point to the extent that you are oblivious to what is happening in the here and now. (Review the section on "Substitutions" in Chapter 7 for more examples of how to use your personal experiences to create deeper empathy with your character.)

EXERCISES

Review Chapter 7 for help with these exercises.

CHANGING THE FILTER

Select a scene you haven't prepared and choose a character to explore. Read into a tape recorder the other character's lines leaving spaces between for your lines. Now, commit to a point of view for your character and anchor the belief in action.

Imagine that one of your lines is: "Who do you think you are?" You have decided that your point of view is: "No one ever gave me anything. I worked hard for everything I've got." (Remember to anchor the belief in action by supplying specific events.) Now, play back your cue and respond with your lines. When you finish, rewind the tape for step two. Choose a different point of view, anchor it, then turn on the recorder again. As you hear the other character's lines the second time, mark the difference in what the other person *seems* to be saying. (Note that I am not advising you to check your interpretation of *your* lines, or your emotions. Instead, notice how differently you perceive the other person's sentiments when they come to you through a changed filter system.)

Compare this web of filters you create to the filters we use for modifying the lighting on a stage set. Place one colored gel in front of the lighting instrument and the light takes on a soft, warm, rosy glow. Another gel causes the same light to produce a cool and sharp effect, with a hint of blue. With no gel, the light may appear flat and uninteresting. When you define your given circumstances, you are creating filters through which you perceive the action and if you change the filters you will get different results.

MOVE THE LAND MINES

Read this short scene with a partner and play character A.

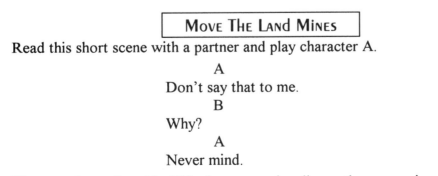

A
Don't say that to me.
B
Why?
A
Never mind.

You may have found it difficult to get a handle on the scene since it is deliberately ambiguous. Before playing the scene again, define your given circumstances. First, define your relationship with B. ("Someone in my family," is not a useful answer. Decide exactly who B is. Perhaps you are talking to your father and your relationship with him has not been ideal—an older sister or brother always seems to please him more.) Second, where are you? ("At home" won't do—be specific. Are you in the house where you, the character, grew up? Are you sitting at the dining room table where you have eaten hundreds of family meals?) Third, define "that." (Exactly what did B say to you? "He was mean to me" isn't enough—your answer must be specific. Perhaps he said, "I liked your hair better before you cut it.") When you read the scene again it no longer seems ambiguous. Words that were empty now resonate with meaning.

Before you read the scene again, make one change in your character's world. For example, move the scene to a party where you are surrounded by close friends, or *remember* that your father was the one who suggested your hair was too long. Now the words have taken on new meanings. Read the scene several times changing the circumstances each time (the possibilities for choices are limited only by your imagination) and notice the variety in resonance.

Remember What Happened

Tape-record a five-or-six-line monologue *before* defining the given circumstances. Postpone listening to your work. Create a vivid and detailed *remember when* for a specific line in the monologue. (See Chapter 2 for help with *remember when's*.) For example, if your character refers to last year's family picnic, use your imagination to go back in time and visit that picnic. *Remember* the sights, sounds, smells, tastes, and the physical sensations. *See* the giant oaks and the red and white tablecloth on the ground. *Hear* the laughing and squealing children and the river lapping against the bank. *Smell* the hot dogs cooking on the grill; *taste* the cold lemonade; and *feel* the hot summer breeze on your skin. What were you doing? Determine the physical activity (playing Frisbee) and the dramatic action (trying to patch up things with your sister). Now, record the monologue a second time. Listen to the two recordings and note the added resonance when you refer to the picnic. Finally, *fill up* all the lines, record the entire monologue, then listen to all three versions of the work.

Using Substitutions

Select a three-or-four-line speech in which your character refers to an off-stage character. Delay making a substitution for the character you talk about. Read the monologue, tape recording your work. (Review Chapter 7 for more information on using substitutions.) Before you listen to your work, make a substitution, then record the piece a second time. Avoid laboring to call up pictures of your substitution. Trust your character's memory. When you listen to the two renderings of the speech, note the impact produced by the substitution. Experiment with various substitutions.

You must not try to play the given circumstances. You may be tempted to monitor the character's memory—demanding recall of *appropriate* images at predetermined moments. If you fall into that trap, however, you will show us the actor at work. After all, in real life, you would never *try* to remember an event or a relationship with the purpose of producing an emotional response, so don't manipulate your character into unnatural behavior. Define the character's context then let go and allow yourself to experience the pressure of the framework you have created. **When you commit to a particular set of**

circumstances, you can rely on that context to provoke needs, and those needs will, in turn, evoke actions. Use the preparation period to provide your character memories, then, during the playing, focus your attention outside yourself. Rely on the interchange between yourself and the other characters to be the friction that sparks those memories. Trust your exquisite and intricate design of connections to affect each successive moment and you will be on your way to allowing the part to play you.

A man of words and not of deeds
Is like garden full of weeds.
                              Anonymous: Nursery Rhyme

What you do speaks so loud that I cannot hear what you say.
Ralph Waldo Emerson

Chapter 14

PLAYING THE ACTION

Actions Speak Louder Than Words

Having imagined a past and accepted the character's state of affairs as if it were your own, you must be willing to behave accordingly. In other words, rather than trying to display your circumstances, you should reveal them through your actions. Exercises in the last chapter demonstrated this principle. When you unconditionally devote your physical and mental energies to fulfilling the desires motivated by your imagined circumstances, you will be compelled to *do* and you will exploit every possibility to accomplish your objectives. For example, if your father stung you by criticizing your new haircut, you were compelled to respond. You may have used your words to strike him, warn him, or beg him for mercy. At any event, you reacted or acted in opposition to your father's action. It is this interaction that most interests your audience—they came to see what *happens*, or what people do to one another. They want to see how this story turns out. Will your father apologize and, if he does, will you forgive him? Will this exchange drive the two of you further apart?

Anytime you place actor-business at the center of your awareness, rather than character-business, you fail to tell your character's story. If you have told yourself that what other people think of your performance is more important than the performance itself, you will be desperate to display all your actor skills. You will be tempted to dedicate too much of your mental and physical energy to actor-tasks. You will focus on remembering lines, making the correct crosses, and registering what you think are appropriate emotional responses. Since you are immersed in actor-circumstances, you are experiencing actor-needs, thus executing actor-actions. If someone criticizes you, in this case, for not playing the action, you may easily recognize that you have been sidetracked by actor-needs.

In some instances, however, you may find the criticism confusing. Perhaps you received notes that you failed to listen and dropped out of character. The next run-through you put those concerns uppermost in your mind, worked hard at correcting your mistakes and still got negative comments. Paying attention to listening and trying to stay in character may appear to be the ideal goal. But if you are thinking about listening and staying in character, you are still paying more attention to actor-needs than character-needs. It's true you are *doing* a great deal and you are reacting, since you are responding to and correcting your imagined mistakes or celebrating perceived victories. Despite all that, you are still showing the audience only actor-doing and, since it is the doing that reveals the story, you are revealing what is happening to you, the actor, and this script isn't your story.

The audience wants to follow the character's story and that is possible only if you are willing to execute the character's actions. Don't *show* us your character and don't fill your mind with self-talk reminding you to stay in character. Take care of the character's concerns and, by your doing, you will reveal the character. Don't show us your action. If you notice that you are playing action, then you are no longer doing it. Your character isn't aware of "playing action." Don't show the audience how a person listens—listen. Don't show the audience your character's needs—fight to satisfy them. Don't show us how your character feels—struggle to solve your character-problems in spite of your feelings. Be ruthlessly honest in your work. Abandon mind, body, and spirit to the fulfillment of the character's needs; otherwise, the character is mindless, has no flesh and is without a soul.

SCOREKEEPING

Just as identifying action during preparation helps point you toward *doing,* an awareness of scorekeeping may help you stay anchored in the character's action. For example, in the scene where you are struggling to persuade your brother to sign the contract, you realize on a moment-to-moment basis whether your tactics are succeeding or failing. Are you able to sway him with your arguments, or is he stubbornly refusing to budge? If you are losing, you will be angry, sad, or confused and you will scramble to change your course of action. If you are winning him over, you celebrate. If he stung you with what he just said, you may try to swat him; however, unless you keep score you won't know whether or not your aim was accurate.

Scorekeeping is not a new technique you need to acquire—you have been doing it all your life. Without giving yourself special instructions, you consciously or unconsciously respond to each action's success or failure. If you toss a dart at a target on the wall, you note how close you got to the bull's-eye and, before you take your next toss, you adjust your aim accordingly. You do this naturally because you have been using this technique of processing information and adjusting tactics since you were an infant. If you attend to character needs, you will keep score. Only a preoccupation with actor-needs can block out the character's desires and inhibit this natural thought process. Pay attention to whether you are succeeding or failing. Scorekeeping is a vital part of communication.

EXERCISES

Review Chapters 7, 8, and 9, "Defining The Given Circumstances," "Discovering The Dramatic Action," and "Identifying The Revelations," before doing these exercises.

MORE LAND MINES

Prepare to read this scene with a partner and play character A.

> A
> Tell me the truth.
> B
> I am.
> A
> Oh, really.

Ask yourself: What is the relationship, where are you, what makes you think this person may be lying, and what happens immediately before you speak? Perhaps you are with your lover on a moonlit walk along the beach. You know he or she loves to tease you and the line you imagine hearing, just before you speak is, "I have tickets for Acapulco." Now read the scene and tape-record the reading. When you listen, note the actions you are playing. Create a different set of circumstances and read the scene again. For example, imagine you are talking to a five-year-old who is trying to convince you that the cookies in his hand didn't come from the open cookie jar on the counter. Devise several sets of circumstances making them only slightly different, then completely different, and afterwards note the actions.

GET OUT YOUR TOOL KIT

Keep in mind that words are tools meant to help you *get the job done*. Choose different *jobs* and use the first line of this short scene to *get the job done*. For example, you might use these words to yank on the person's sleeve, or to push him or her against the wall, or to lick his or her boots. Visualize yourself carrying out the action as you say the words.

As a rule, when you consciously dedicate your mental and physical energies to the execution of an action, you will unconsciously create circumstances that support your action. For example, if you decide that you will use the words to yank at the other character's sleeve, you will create a relationship for which that action would be appropriate. You might find yourself talking to your best friend. If, instead, you use the words to slam the person against the wall, you will probably imagine an enemy.

> A
> I need an answer.
> B
> You got it.
> A
> No way.

See how many actions you can play with this first line and make the choices as different as possible. Experiment with outrageous choices.

CATCH THE PROS DOING IT

Use your VCR to view a well-made movie and pay close attention to the dramatic action in each scene. View a scene several times scoring the action, line by line, for each character.

CREATING AN OBSTACLE COURSE

Tape-record yourself and another actor reading this scene. Play character A.

> A
> Have you got it?
> B
> Uh-huh.
> A
> Give it to me.

Identify "it." Are you referring to the television remote control or the overdue utility bill? Are you talking about a competitor's business plan or the filed-down spoon you are using to tunnel out of a prison cell? Be specific. Create a set of circumstances. For the sake of comparison later, don't establish any obstacles between you and what you want. Imagine that B is going to meet your demands because he or she always does. Record the scene but, before you listen to your work, place obstructions in your path. *Remember* that B has sworn never to give "it" up, swearing to protect "it" with his or her life. Read the scene again after you commit to overcoming the obstacle. Imagine other difficulties: you promised you would never ask; you are asking a sworn enemy; you must not be overheard by the occupants of the next room. Now read the scene committing to each choice in turn. After you have experimented with several obstacles, listen to your work and notice how the struggle adds to the intensity of the playing.

RAISING THE STAKES

Continue to work on the scene used in "Creating An Obstacle Course" and explore the effect of raising the stakes. First read the scene without considering the stakes, then devise answers to: *What will happen if I fail?* and *What will I gain if I succeed?* Make your answers vivid and deeply personal. Experiment with several scenarios. Read the scene knowing that "it" is worth a million dollars, then as if it were virtually worthless. Read the scene knowing that if you are heard by the people in the next room, you will be executed. Then get B to give "it" to you because you need it to complete your homework assignment. After you have experimented with several choices, listen to your work and notice how much raising or lowering the stakes affects action.

FIND THE METAPHOR

Using any of the scenes you have already worked on, describe the action with a metaphor such as cat-and-mouse, courting dance, sword fight, tennis match, chess game, boxing match, or pillow fight. Record the exercise several times, after having steeped the scene in one of these images, and when you listen notice the rich, new nuances that you have brought into your work.

KEEP SCORE

Watch the movie you studied for "Catch The Pros Doing It" and observe the score-keeping done by the characters. Notice their responses to points scored and points lost. Observe the power shifts.

Walk Into The Ambush

Identify the revelations in your script. Experiment, for example, with the scene in Chapter 9. Play the scene, first knowing all the information in advance, then expecting the opposites. Notice that when you experience the moments of discovery, you encounter more problems and the difficulties instigate action.

If you commit to satisfying your character-needs, you take most of the strain out of acting—you free yourself from actor-struggles. Focusing on doing helps you avoid actor traps such as showing your feelings, trying to demonstrate given circumstances, or displaying a character. **When you direct your physical and mental energies to solving the character's problems you can trust yourself to behave spontaneously and allow the part to play you.**

What is character but the determination of incident? What is incident but the illustration of character?

Henry James, *The Art Of Fiction*

It is easier to manufacture seven facts out of
whole cloth than one emotion.

Mark Twain

CHAPTER 15

FEELINGS

As Shy As Wild Animals

Nothing gets in the way of commendable acting more than a preoccupation with feelings. In real life you would never think, "I need to feel angry at this moment." Still, actors regularly sabotage their performances by trying to supervise their emotions. Some actors think they can command emotions to appear or make themselves display emotions that they aren't experiencing. These misguided actors defy human nature.

In your daily interactions with people, you might want to punish someone who hurt you and you might think, "I want you to suffer for what you did to me." Your pulse may be pounding, your eyes narrowed and your entire body tense with fury. But you most certainly would not be directing yourself to feel angry, nor would you be thinking about ways to display rage. Your attention would be on the interaction between yourself and the other person. In real life, if people make a show of their emotions we recognize the hypocrisy. You notice the sham when a person tries too hard to prove he is happy to see you. When a person acts as if everything is fine, even though she clearly is upset, you don't fall for the pretense. If you are happy to see someone, you would immediately see the absurdity of directing yourself to parade the joy you feel. **Your only motivation for *showing* an emotion is a desire to hoodwink others. You use this tactic when you want to convince someone that you are experiencing emotions other than those you genuinely feel.**

Instead of placing yourself in this predicament, use tactics that will generate authentic emotions. Immerse yourself in the character's given circumstances and genuinely pursue the character's intentions, then you can expect to employ appropriate actions and the success or failure of those actions will produce emotional responses. If you focus on character-concerns, you will produce character-responses and your feelings will be character-feelings. **Emotions are by-products of action. You cannot play feelings; you can play actions and trust that the results of those actions will produce feelings.**

When people interact with one another, their primary concern is to satisfy their physical and mental needs. More often than not, they try to keep their emotions out of the way so they can concentrate on problem solving. In other words, people carry on in spite of their feelings. How different this is from the actor who forgets all about what the character wants and focuses on showing us how the character *feels* about those needs. Certainly people do frequently hide their emotions by pretending to feel something other than their true emotions. If, however, you are managing your emotions, while performing, it had better be your character's action not an actor-action. If you, as the character, are hiding the pain inflicted on you by another character—that might be part of the action in the scene. But, if you, the actor, are attempting to conjure up what you think is the correct emotion—that qualifies only as bad acting.

Luring Your Emotions

If you accept the statement that you cannot play feelings and you vow to never again manipulate your emotions, your resolve will be tested often. The script may specifically call for certain feelings and, as if that weren't enough, directors often give result direction that calls for a particular emotion. While you need not blatantly ignore notations in the script and it wouldn't be prudent to mentally thumb your nose at the director, don't let these directives tempt you to be dishonest in your work. Instead, follow the advice Stanislavski gave his students:

> Our artistic emotions are, at first, as shy as wild animals and
> they hide in the depths of our souls. If they do not come to
> the surface spontaneously, you cannot go after them. All
> you can do is to concentrate your attention on the most ef-
> fective kind of lure for them.[1]

Choosing The Bait

Let's look at an example of how you might lure your emotions. Your line is: "No one told me she would be here." The writer has included the direction "seething with anger" and the actor playing your aunt, to whom you have spoken, responds with "I knew you would be angry." The director has said, "I really need you to be angry here." Remember that although you can't mandate an emotion, you may entice the emotion with the right bait.

Begin by creating *remember when's* that fill your character's mental suitcase with images. Imagine that the last time your sister attended a family gathering, she called your mother a penny-pincher, blaming your parents for her financial woes. She carried on the assault until your mother left the room in tears. When you criticized your sister's behavior, she humiliated you in front of everyone by describing, in merciless detail, your troubled love life. Then, she accused you of squandering her inheritance and undermining her relationship with your parents.

Take advantage of your substitution technique. Make this an intensely personal issue. How does your character's situation parallel an experience from your past? Who in your life has failed to take responsibility for personal predicaments? Who has blamed you for his or her own failures? Who has hurt someone you love in a selfish attempt to justify his or her fiascoes? Who has put you through ordeals that have left you seething with anger and resentment? *Cast* that person as your sister. What did that person do and how did you react? Keep in mind that what is most significant about your experience is what it caused you to *do*, since you can only play actions, never feelings.

For more information on using substitutions effectively, review Chapters 7 and 13. Remember the *formula*: Commit to the given circumstances; play the action; and sustain an uninterrupted exchange of actions, thoughts, and feelings with the other actors. When you work this way you will free your unconscious mind to intuitively make numerous substitutions. On the occasions when you consciously make substitutions, keep your choices simple, immediate and heartfelt. Complete your preparation, then let it go. Trust that, while you are playing the action, the events occurring in the character's present moments will trigger mental images, and those images will evoke emotional responses.

After committing to your *remember when's* and your substitutions, you have reason to expect that when you learn your sister will join the family for dinner tonight the news will affect you. Even so, the most thorough preparation imaginable will fail you if, during the scene, you choose the wrong target for the center of your concentration. When you hear your cue, you must not watch to see whether the anger rises in you. At the moment you check on yourself, you step out of the action and you begin to play director. What's more, in chasing the emotion, you will frighten away the "wild animals." You must trust that you have properly baited the trap and rely on your preparation. Play the action. Never try to feel anything.

Even if, when the scene is over, the director says, "No, no, I think you should be much angrier when you learn your sister has been invited," all you can do is sweeten the bait before the next run-through. You might intensify the details of your *remember when*. You could imagine that your sister squandered most of the family fortune, then, when you pitied her and took her into your business, her mismanagement of funds bankrupted your company. As if that weren't enough, you caught her in lies about your spouse. You might return to your substitution. Plunge deeper into the heart of that experience. Keep poking around in the details of those events, focusing on doing, until you *strike a nerve*.

Don't Get Attached To Results

The new specifics provided by your preparation will *probably* make your blood boil when you hear that you must again confront your nemesis. Keep in mind, however, that you can never guarantee that the anger will arrive on cue. Don't focus on results. Remember that emotions are by-products of action, actions are the results of needs, and needs arise out of circumstances. You must not start "at the wrong end." Since your emotions will never be within your direct control, pay attention, during preparation, to what you can manage: choices regarding your character's circumstances, needs, and actions. While performing, direct your energy toward solving your character's problems. Then, be patient and remain truthful in your work. Regardless of how thoroughly you have prepared and how focused you are on action, it's possible that, at the moment of truth, you won't deliver the prescribed anger. But if you experience a profound moment of interaction and touch us with your simplicity, clarity and authenticity, no one will mourn the absence of anger. Bear in mind that the audience hasn't read the author's notes and didn't hear your director's instructions. The audience will find a way to justify your aunt's comment about your anger. They will chalk it up to her inability to interpret your response. They probably will find the incongruity fascinatingly human. The audience prefers authenticity over formulaic work. Never try to force-feed them synthetic emotions.

Bring Your Own Feelings To Your Work

Have you ever tried to stifle an emotion you found unpleasant? Have you attempted to substitute what you regarded as an appropriate emotion for a feeling you decided the character shouldn't have? Perhaps you were experiencing fear. Your hands were sweating, you were short of breath and your logical mind insisted that your character wouldn't be afraid in this scene. It's natural to want to rid yourself of such unpleasant sensations. If you manage to wall off the fear and steel yourself against the physical sensations, you may welcome the numbness that results. You may believe that your maneuver was successful.

Here is the rub. Yes, you have succeeded in ridding yourself of the pesky symptoms of fear. What you are left with, on the other hand, is impassivity, a sense of being disconnected and perhaps even bored. Your acting, then, will be spiritless because suppressing your feelings has left you lifeless. **If you have no life, neither does the character.** In the interest of emotional safety, you have shut yourself off from disturbing sensations, and you have turned yourself into a virtual zombie. In this shutdown condition, you will be especially vulnerable to result acting. Since you have rendered yourself impassive, you will find it particularly tempting to manipulate yourself into what you hope are appropriate emotional responses.

Always Act In Your Own Person

Never disconnect from your feelings. Instead, let into your consciousness the discomfort of character needs; focus your attention outside yourself; commit to the doing; and permit the character free access to all your emotions. This is what Stanislavski referred to when he said:

> Never lose yourself on the stage. Always act in your own person, as an artist. You can never get away from yourself. The moment you lose yourself on the stage marks the departure from truly living your part and the beginning of exaggerated false acting. Therefore, no matter how much you act, how many parts you take, you should never allow your-

self any exception to the rule of using your own feelings. To break that rule is the equivalent of killing the person you are portraying, because you deprive him of a palpitating, living, human soul, which is the real source of life for a part.[2]

Allow your character to roam your consciousness, choosing freely from your emotional cupboard as he or she requires. Stop editing. Don't dole out stingy little tidbits that you have approved. If you lack the courage to make all your feelings available, you will starve your character.

WHAT ABOUT NERVES?

I doubt there is an actor alive who hasn't dealt with performance anxiety. Like everyone else who has suffered from an attack of nerves, you know that anxiety can wreck your performance. If you hope to cope with this problem, you need to develop tactics. It should be clear by now that shutting down or smothering awareness of the anxiety isn't a viable option.

One of your most powerful weapons in dealing with nerves is understanding the source for your anxiety. Look first to your inner dialogue. Actor-thoughts will, naturally, produce actor-responses just as character-thoughts will produce character-responses. If your heart is thumping madly and you are having trouble breathing, it's because of what you were thinking. You may have said to yourself: "This scene is never going to work; it hasn't worked yet" or "The critics loved this scene last night. Oh, boy, I'd better do exactly what I did then." In this condition, you are doomed to a shoddy performance. Because your actor-thoughts produced the anxiety, the best solution is to change your thinking. Replace your actor-need for approval with your character-needs, then dedicate your physical and mental power to satisfying your character's requirements. Replace the anxiety producing actor-thoughts about performance and critic's reviews with character-thoughts about other characters and character-needs.

Should focusing on character-concerns fail to calm your anxiety, you have no other viable choice but to justify the feelings you are experiencing. **Ultimately, the only feelings you have to work with are the feelings you are actually experiencing at the moment.** For example, in a situation like the one just described you might use justification in the following manner. "Why shouldn't I be scared? If I don't persuade this man to give me the information I need, my son will die." Your feelings haven't changed; nevertheless, by assigning the emotions to the character, you have eliminated an actor-dilemma and left yourself free to get on with character-business. Shutting down is never the solution.

Another way to ensure that you begin your work free of paralyzing anxiety is to use relaxation exercises. This allows you to catch your breath—both literally and figuratively. Be careful, however, that you don't become engrossed in the actor-desire to relax and lose sight of the character-concerns. After relieving your tension, promptly transfer your attention to the character's needs. If you immediately return to your actor *what if's,* you probably will revert to the state of anxiety. Don't waste the time you spent on relaxation.

TRUST THE MIND—BODY LINK

You learned in Chapter 4 that emotions are in your body, not just in your head. Feelings are not just ideas; they are visceral experiences. For example, imagine yourself at an audition. You are thinking: "Oh, no, I'm not right for this part—I know they want someone younger (or older)," or "I wish I had done more preparation," or "I hope I remember my lines." Your thoughts will produce anxiety and that anxiety will be in your body, not just in your mind. Your hands will get clammy; your breathing will become shallow; and you will stop producing sufficient saliva. It is impossible to limit emotions to your mind. They will spill out and into your body. This occurs, not because you order it with your conscious mind but, because of the mind-body link that functions without your conscious control.

Once you allow yourself to be genuinely affected by what is happening to you, you may feel obligated to display your feelings. Don't worry. Your body will reveal your responses. Your eyes, your mouth, tiny muscles all over your face, your hands, your feet, your shoulders—all will reflect your emotions unless you get in the way. Similarly, when the emotions you think you *must* experience don't appear as commanded (and, of course, if commanded, they never do), you may believe you need to *indicate*. You may try to show the emotion you think you should be feeling, whether you are feeling it or not. If you make that blunder, your audience will see a person trying to *act out* a feeling, not a person *experiencing* a feeling. The difference between the two is vast and your audience won't be fooled for a moment. Attempting to show us how the character feels by imitating emotional responses (forcing a laugh, drawing your face into a frown) produces acting that is difficult to watch on stage and almost impossible to watch on film. Instead, place yourself inside the character's skin so that you end up experiencing the emotions, then leave it up to your audience to make the interpretations and label the feelings.

DEMOLISH SOME MISGUIDED IDEAS ABOUT EMOTIONS

DISTINGUISH BETWEEN EMOTIONS AND ATTITUDES

There is a difference between emotional responses and intellectual adjustments to feelings. You *feel* mad, glad, sad, afraid, hurt, loving, surprised, ashamed, or disgusted. You may *respond* to your feeling by affecting an attitude that is hostile, sarcastic, approval-seeking, contemptuous, bored, etc. These responses are habitual ways of dealing with your feelings—they are not feelings. Indeed, the primary function of attitudes is to protect you from emotions. If you fail to establish contact with your emotions and persistently substitute attitudes for feelings, your characters will be cold and bloodless. This result is inevitable because, by focusing on intellectual adjustments, you have engaged your mind but left your body detached.

Avoid Labels

Avoid oversimplifying emotions by attaching labels. Rarely do we feel pure emotions. More often than not what we experience is a complex cluster of emotions that consists of many feelings layered and woven together. I have seen actors torture themselves trying to accurately determine what the character is feeling at a particular moment. You aren't hired to identify emotions or to describe them. Your job is to make yourself a conduit through which emotions flow. Labels are often limiting. Keep in mind that the moment you drag your emotions up to a certain level of consciousness, they lose their authenticity. Once you pin them down, you have something resembling the feeling but not the feeling itself. Stay focused on the lures you established and keep your character's concerns uppermost in your mind. If there is any labeling of passions to be done, leave that to the audience.

Fall In Love With Action, Rather Than Emotions

Because most actors are creatures of great passion, many of them are what I call *feeling junkies*. In other words, they believe that emotions are the be all and end all of acting. If you fall in that category, you may have trouble keeping your attention off your feelings while you work. You may be in love with your emotions. Occasionally, I see scenes that don't work because the actors are so busy admiring their passions that they have no time to pursue actions. You mustn't ride herd on your emotions, trying to control what you experience. Conversely, neither should you get caught admiring your emotional gymnastics. Trust that your pursuit of action will result in the by-product of emotions and leave it to the audience to appreciate your work.

EXERCISES

Use the exercises from Chapters 13 and 14 to explore methods for luring your emotions. For example, execute "Move The Land Mines" in Chapter 13 several times, changing the circumstances each run-through. When you listen to your work, you will notice that the choices have produced definite changes in your emotions. While some of the differences are subtle, others are dramatic. When you alter the character's circumstances, you affect the character's needs. Those needs will demand certain kinds of action and the exchange of actions between characters will result in feelings. Make some choices with the intent of producing particular emotions. (Refer to "Luring Your Emotions" in this chapter.) Remember that your body should react to the information you give yourself. Does your jaw tighten? Do your eyes sting? Does a laugh come up from your belly? If your choices don't affect you physically as you devise them, don't expect them to suddenly work for you when you are playing the scene.

Keep these principles in mind when you act:

☞ **Always concern yourself with what you need to *do*, never with what you need to feel.**

☞ **Follow Stanislavski's advice and "Always act in your own person."**

☞ **Trust that when you experience emotions, your experience is sufficient. You never have to concern yourself with showing us what you are feeling.**

In no other facet of your work is the advice to allow the part to play you more valuable. Because you cannot mandate an emotion, you must hone your skills until you can effectively entice these "wild animals." Then, you must resolutely resist the temptation to pursue them if they do not rise to the bait. **Even when you suffer the most severe frustration because your feelings seem to "hide in the depths" of your soul, you must direct your energies to solving the character's problems. Trust that the degree of success or failure you experience during that character quest will produce authentic emotional responses.**

FOOTNOTES

[1]Constantin Stanislavski, *An Actor Prepares*, p. 180.
[2]Constantin Stanislavski, p. 167.

My words fly up, my thoughts
remain below:
Words without thoughts never to heaven go.
William Shakespeare, *Hamlet*

CHAPTER 16

STAYING IN CHARACTER

Thinking The Character's Thoughts

Staying in character means placing your character-needs ahead of your actor-needs. It means directing your energy—physical and mental—into solving character-problems and overcoming the character's obstacles. If you are in character, you will fight the character's battles and think character-thoughts. You will not have time for actor-battles and actor-thoughts.

It's common knowledge that, while you may quickly learn to speak a foreign language, for a time you continue to think in your native tongue. An actor must quickly learn to speak the character's words *and* think the character's thoughts. This is the "inner intensity" Stanislavski talks about when he says the actor "may sit without a motion and at the same time be in full action."[1] Without this inner activity, the thought process, your character is some kind of science fiction creature. The creature walks and talks like a human being, yet obviously isn't human, since it doesn't think.

You may believe you have stepped into character when, in truth, you have only begun to think more about your performance. In that case, your inner dialogue will go something like this: "I hope this scene is working." "I hope it goes as well as it did last time." "Wait! Why isn't this other actor doing what she should be doing?" "Is this where I am supposed to cross?" "Oh, no! What's my next line?" "How am I ever going to get through that marathon monologue?" "Whoops! Here comes the speech where I'm supposed to cry/laugh/sigh/swoon/giggle/explode/frown/fidget/etc., etc." "I have to remember to listen. What did she just say?" While you think these thoughts, the character doesn't exist, because, during those moments, the character has no mind.

You must learn to set aside your actor-needs and, instead, direct your attention to solving your character's problems. When your actions are motivated by your character's needs, you will pay attention to the other characters and their actions. Then, your inner dialogue will focus on the other characters and it will sound more like this: "Why don't you listen to me?" "You always have an excuse don't you?" "How can you say that to me?" "I wish I deserved that adoration I see in your eyes." "How do I convince you how awful the outcome of all this will be, if you don't listen to me?" "Why can't I make you understand what I am feeling right now?" "How many times do I have to explain this to you?" When you use your mind to consider, ponder, remember, or anticipate character-concerns, you will involve the viewers in the character's story.

Stepping Into Character

The moment before you step into character, your actor-needs still fill the center of your awareness. The transition, during which you attempt to dislodge actor-thoughts and replace them with the character-concerns, is not always an easy one. Just before the director says, "Action," or before you walk from the wings onto the stage, your actor-self is screaming for continued attention. Like a spoiled child, the performer part of you yanks at the sleeve of your mind, certain that only actor-needs matter. ("Oh, no. What's the first line of that long monologue on the second page?" "I can't wait to bring down the house when I hit that punch line at the end of the scene.") Your character-self, on the other hand, doesn't even whisper in your ear to remind you of problems, regardless of how pressing those predicaments may be. While your actor-self needles you incessantly to satisfy aspirations, the character-self imposes no such requirements.

Only by an act of will can you turn a deaf ear to the relentless demands of the actor-self. It is not necessarily natural to devote your energies to solving the problems of the character-self, when the character is silent, demanding nothing. This is why you must develop concentration and imagination. By using your imagination, you are able to make the character's cravings more urgent, more fascinating, more demanding than your actor-concerns. Because concentration follows interest, you will then be able to focus your attention on the character's difficulties. If you continue to have trouble staying in character, re-read Chapters 2 and 3 and use the exercises to improve your concentration and imagination.

Don't Get Caught Acting

It's tempting to believe you can think about some actor problems while you work because you have been told over and over that you should be doing these things when you act. After a performance, the director (or an assistant) usually gives you notes including comments about listening, crossing left two lines earlier, concentrating, remembering your lines, or playing the action. Nevertheless, since those are actor-concerns, they must live only in that area of peripheral awareness discussed in Chapter 1. You must relegate the actor-concerns to the automatic mind just as you would the mechanics of driving your car or riding your bicycle.

The actor-concerns that are most apt to lure you come under the heading of "My character would never do that." You may believe that you have to watch yourself, being certain that you don't behave in a way that is inconsistent with the choices you committed to during your preparation. If you have appointed yourself a member of the acting police, your inner dialogue will reflect your concerns. You will entertain thoughts such as these: "She would never sit like this." "I don't think I should get angry here. He would never let her see his anger." "She would be more understanding. My feelings of impatience must be a sign I have dropped out of character." Joining the acting police is the sure way to a performance that is stilted and predictable. Leave room in your performance for surprises and eccentricities. It is the inconsistencies that add fascinating texture to the portrayal. They will delight the audience and tickle their imaginations. Characters who are totally consistent do not seem fully human.

Don't Go Off The Deep End

Rest assured that this advice to fill the center of your awareness with character concerns does not imply that you lose all touch with actual reality. We don't want Othello to actually strangle Desdemona every night. Staying in character means you hold character needs at the center of your awareness and allow actor needs to shift to the periphery of consciousness.

If **any** actor concerns occupy the center of your awareness during the playing, you are no longer playing the character. **If you are preoccupied with listening, concentrating, remembering when to make the cross or what your next line is, or even *trying* to stay in character, you can't be in character.** What the audience will see is not the character involved in an action, but an actor at work. Although the audience may credit you with being a conscientious actor who remembers lines and crosses and tries hard to listen, that is not what they came to see. They came to witness a story played out and have no particular interest in watching an actor's display of craftsmanship. Resist all temptation to mentally stand outside the character's experience and observe yourself playing the role. While wearing the character's shoes, use your mind to solve the character's problems. Play the dramatic action, and let the part play you.

FOOTNOTES
---
[1]Constantin Stanislavski, *An Actor Prepares*, p. 34.

Ecstasy is the accurate term for the intensity of consciousness that occurs in the creative act. But it is not to be thought of merely as a Bacchic 'letting go'; it involves the total person, with the subconscious and unconscious acting in unity with the conscious. It is not, thus, *irrational*; it is rather, suprarational. It brings intellectual, volitional, and emotional functions into play all together.

Rollo May, *The Courage To Create*

He'd fly through the air with the greatest of ease,
This daring young man on the flying trapeze;
His movements were graceful, all the girls he could please,
And My love he purloined away!
George Leybourne, *The Man on the Flying Trapeze*

CHAPTER 17

LET GO AND FLY

The purpose of preparation is to give you the confidence to work spontaneously without inhibition. Its purpose is to set free your creative spirit. You must not use it as means of confining your spirit. You must not turn the preparation into a method of insuring that you won't make mistakes. Your preparation is not a weight you mentally drag around behind you, or tie around your neck, or push up a hill in front of you. It is meant to be a framework that supports your creative efforts.

Be certain that your groundwork is complete. Work tirelessly and consistently at honing all your basic skills. Never stop growing as an artist. Behave professionally, take your work seriously—although not necessarily solemnly. Never permit yourself work that is careless or less than your best. Plunge wholeheartedly into the process by which you offer yourself to the character you are about to reveal. Devour the script during the exploration period. Determine the given circumstances, discover the dramatic action, identify the revelations. Make choices that are specific, detailed, rich, imaginative, fearless, and deeply personal. *But* be certain that you clearly recognize the moment when you shift from preparation to execution. When you are allowing the character to play you, you must free yourself to have the character's experience. While getting ready, you attended to actor-concerns. When you are on-stage, or in front of the camera, it is time for character-concerns.

As constructive as the groundwork can be, it is only useful if it provides a framework within which you are liberated. If you constantly fret over your framework during performance, you convert it into a destructive force. Don't turn your preparation into hobbles—it is meant to provide you with wings.

EMBRACE THE TENSION BETWEEN LIMITATIONS AND FREEDOM
Creativity springs from the tension between limitations and freedom. The form (stage, film, TV), the writer, the director, the physical setting, other actors and even your

costume will provide some obvious restrictions. You will have memorized words to re-peat, a time to say them, and certain physical actions to perform. Some limitations will be of your own devising—when you commit to your choices regarding given circumstances, needs and revelations, you create a clearly defined framework within which you must function. (For example, if, during your preparation, you chose to *remember* that your father abused you as a child, that imagined fact will shape your response to certain behavior and inhibit some feelings.)

While all these limitations are essential to the effectiveness of your playing, it is equally necessary that you liberate yourself to improvise within those boundaries when you begin to play. **If your work is to be truthful, you must give yourself permission to think, feel and behave with total spontaneity within your established limitations.** The freedom to be spontaneous, unpredictable, even irrational—within the boundaries established by form, direction and personal choices—is the secret to genuinely creative acting.

Immediately before the scene begins you must let go of your preparation and plunge into the character's circumstances. You must trust that, with your groundwork, you have built a solid and dependable framework within which you are free to improvise. The free-dom to improvise is crucial. You must be bold enough to believe that your thorough preparation will sustain you—that you are now beyond the point of making *mistakes*. Af-ter all, you will be too busy stumbling upon new and wonderful possibilities to worry about blunders!

It takes courage to trust your groundwork. On the other hand, if you try to force your preparation to function while you play the piece, you will have to stand outside the experience evaluating and coaching. That makes you a critic, not a doer. You must aban-don yourself to the character's circumstances. **The part will play you only if you play the action; and you will be able to play the action only if you live in the character's present moment.**

Take Flight

Think of your preparation as the rigging and the net that you, the trapeze artist, will depend upon when you electrify us with death-defying stunts of grace and courage. Before you soar through your creative space, thrilling and amazing us, take care of roustabout duties. Set your rigging and safety net firmly in place. Your groundwork is essential. It will support and preserve your creative life force. But roustabouts don't "fly through the air with the greatest of ease." When you let go and take flight toward the person or bar that will prevent you plunging to earth, you had better not be thinking about whether you did an effective job of rigging your support system. When you have completed the appa-ratus that will support you—when the *net* and the *rigging* are secure—it is time to trust and time for you to take flight. Your creative spirit thrives on courage and risk. Trust your preparation and free your spirit to soar.

When writing a novel a writer should create living people;
people not characters. A *character* is a caricature.
Ernest Hemingway, *Death In The Afternoon*, XVI

Chapter 18

THE MISCELLANEOUS FILE

1. **Trust the writing.**
   You don't have to show us anything. Play the action and trust the writing to tell the story, convey the mood, and reveal the character.

2. **Remember: "Less is more."**
   It is wiser to do nothing, allowing the audience to read into your face the emotions they feel are appropriate, than it is to show us what you are feeling and get caught *acting*. Especially when acting for the camera, the actor who "makes faces" is virtually impossible to watch.

3. **You don't have to be clever when talking about acting in order to be an extraordinary actor.**
   It's far more important to play a good game than to talk a good game.

4. **Carefully listen to the direction or criticism you receive and incorporate the suggestions into what you are already doing. Although it may be tempting, you should never throw out everything and start over.**
   Compare the preparation you have done to having cooked a pot of stew. You spent a great deal of time chopping and slicing meat and vegetables and seasoning the ingredients. It took more time for the meat and vegetables to cook. Finally, you have tasted the stew and you are pleased with your culinary accomplishment. Perhaps fifteen minutes before mealtime someone suggests the dish could use a little more basil. Although you might decide to follow the suggestion, you certainly wouldn't throw out everything and begin with fresh water, raw meat and uncleaned vegetables—not if you are going to eat in a quarter of an hour.

5. **If you suffer nervous tension, you probably are afraid of revealing yourself.**
   Ironically, when you manipulate your emotions in an attempt to shield your true nature, you most clearly expose yourself. Your self-awareness tells us that you are a frightened, insecure actor. Quit trying to disguise yourself. You will, one way or another, reveal yourself to the audience, because you have only your own inner resources to use. You cannot manufacture feelings. You cannot create a new soul, or even a new body.

Eleanora Duse said, "The artist-actor gives the best of himself; through his interpretations, he unveils his inner soul."[1]

6. **Every thought you have is a direction you give yourself.**

If you are thinking "I can't do this scene," you are directing yourself to avoid the experience and your mind, following your instructions, will find ways to disconnect from what is about to happen. (Do you imagine that if a baseball player stands in center field thinking, "I'll never catch this ball," the fielder will then make the catch?) Imagine, on the other hand, you are thinking (as the character) "I have to prevent her from making this horrible mistake." Now, you will direct your energies to the character's task and you will involve yourself in the action of the scene.

7. **Beware of drilling sessions for scenes or monologues.**

You want to avoid habitual performance that gets you in a rut. Allow for new possibilities each run-through. Rediscover the moments each time you work.

8. **Don't become a director.**

The desire for objectivity and analysis burns hotter in your director-mind than in your actor-mind. The director in you may yearn to predetermine exactly what you and other characters should think and feel at each moment. You may not even consciously decide to direct the piece. You may see it in your mind's eye (usually during the first or second reading), then fall in love with the movie in your mind. Don't let that movie seduce you into demonstrating for us the performance you admired. We don't want to watch you *re*-play anything; we want to see the story unfold. I remind my actors that if they are busy directing the piece, who is available to act?

If you get together with fellow performers to rehearse, be on guard against the actor who is a closet director. If there is no bona fide director at the rehearsal, devote the time to running lines, giving your body the opportunity to learn your stage business, and living in your character's skin. Don't be misled by the actor who attempts to debate the suitability of your responses. On the other hand, don't squander valuable time trying to change the work habits of the actor-analyst. Merely agree with whatever this frustrated director has to say, then do whatever you have to do *as the character*.

9. **When you pick up the tempo, don't skip listening.**

When you are directed to pick up the tempo, don't be tempted to rush. You were given this comment because you weren't listening. You were waiting for the other characters to finish speaking before you decided to speak and, in most cases, that is unnatural. Usually your impulse to speak comes while the other character is still talking. Listen for your triggers instead of measuring your tempo.

10. **Remember we speak of an actor *playing* a role, not *working* a role.** Your rehearsal period should be full of play, exploration, improvisation, discovery and experimentation.

FOOTNOTES

[1]Eleanora Duse quoted by Sir John Martin-Harvey, *The Book of Martin-Harvey* (London: H. Walker, Ltd., 1930) pp. 54, 55. Quoted by Cole and Chinoy, *Actors On Acting*.

Trouble has a trick of coming butt end first;
Viewed approaching, then you've seen it at its worst.
Once surmounted, straight it waxes ever small,
And it tapers till there's nothing left at all.
So, whene'er a difficulty may impend,
Just remember you are facing the butt end;
And that looking back upon it, like as not,
You will marvel at beholding just a dot.
Edwin L. Sabin, *Trouble's Strong Front*

CHAPTER 19

YOU ARE UP NEXT ...

DEALING WITH LAST MINUTE PANIC

The curtain is about to go up; or the casting director has just asked, "Are you ready?"; or you are in front of the camera and the assistant director has just said, "Rolling!" And you are stuck. Your mouth is dry. You feel numb. You can't imagine how you are going to survive this experience. You terrified yourself by telling yourself scary stuff, and in an attempt to quell the terror you disconnected from your feelings. Now you are mentally, emotionally and physically paralyzed.

To empty your mind of actor-thoughts and fill it, instead, with character-thoughts, make use of the pink elephant/purple giraffe lesson in Chapter 1, "Learning To Concentrate." This is a concentration challenge pure and simple. Make your character's dreams and fears more fascinating than your own dreams and fears.

One of these techniques may help to make your character's state of affairs more compelling than your own:

- **Take another look at the stakes.**
  Recall what you may lose or what you could gain. Let's assume you have brought your character's circumstances to life. You may have pictured, in vivid detail, how dreadful your future will be if you fail to satisfy your needs. Perhaps, on the other

hand, you have fallen in love with how full and rich life could be *if only* .... Thrusting yourself into one of those character daydreams can catapult you into the mind of the character. Clearly, this works only if the character's stakes are more interesting to you than what you could lose or gain by doing an outstanding job playing the role. Compare this to the bets on the table during a poker game. The *purse* on the character's table will have to mean more to you than the *purse* on the actor's table. If, as the actor, you have bet the family farm, you can't have the character playing for matches.

- **Put the blame on someone new.**
  As the character, blame someone who has gotten you into your difficulty. Imagine yourself telling this villain what you think of him or her for getting you into this mess.

- **Plug into a power source.**
  By touching an object you have previously endowed with special qualities you can re-connect with your character's past and that may fill your mind with character-expectations. Imbue an article of clothing or a prop with meaning for your character. Imagine that the object was given to you by someone very special, or that you were wearing the garment or could touch the object at a crucial moment in your life. Touching that article may flood your consciousness with images and mobilize your character-mind.

- **Add a tangle to the knot.**
  This is particularly useful when the show has already been running awhile or when you are doing the umpteenth take and you can feel your attention wandering. Perhaps, without facing it, you are bored with your character's problems just as you would be with a jigsaw puzzle you have put together too many times. Toss in a new complication. Imagine difficulties you hadn't previously faced.

When your mind is full of character-thoughts—when your character-concerns are more compelling, more immediate, more visceral than actor-concerns—immerse yourself in the moment before. Recall the event that occurred just before this one. Hopefully you have already imagined this event and you have made it vivid and stimulating enough to hold your interest. Enter the character's space filled with the residue of the previous action.

When you are working in front of the camera, you frequently will have to begin scenes mid-action. Especially when you aren't making an entrance and you have the first line, try one of these techniques. Focus your attention on the person you will be working with and, as your character, silently put a question to him or her. Connect the question to the action in the scene and load it emotionally. As you silently project the question to the other character you will find, in the person's eyes, a message that you can treat as a response. Let that response propel you into the action. You could, instead, *hear* what this other person has just said to you and react to that action.

You can see that if you haven't established a foundation none of these techniques will work—they are based on recalling and re-connecting with images you have previously created. Allow yourself however much time you need to prepare for an entrance. By the way, whenever possible (in auditions, or in front of the camera), don't say you are ready until you are ready! Learn to say, "Excuse me, I need a moment."

Auditions

- **Don't try to win the role—claim it.**
  Don't turn auditions into occasions for approval-seeking. The auditors do not want the responsibility for validating your talent; they just hope and pray someone walks through that door who fits the bill. Prepare for the reading; be on time; and, for the auditors, be part of the solution, not part of the problem.

- **To improve your skills as a cold reader do this exercise ten minutes a day.**
  If you absolutely cannot devote ten minutes to the exercise daily, settle for five or even two minutes. Cold reading is an essential skill; set aside *some* time for this work every day.

  Choose something to read other than a script. (Don't act—just read.) Turn the television on, with the sound off. Pay attention to the action on the screen, holding the written material in front of you just low enough so that it doesn't block your view of the screen. Use your thumb to help you mark your place on the page. Look at the page, moving your eyes only, then immediately look up at the action on the screen. Now, say aloud the word, or words, you were able to pick up in that quick glance. You will be tempted to continue looking at the page long enough to read more words than you can retain. Don't. Look down; pick up the words; then look back at the screen and say however many words you have retained. Don't concern yourself with phrasing or interpretation. Stay involved with the action on the screen.

  The purpose of the work isn't improvement of your interpretation skills. With this exercise, you train yourself to see more words at a time. Although in the beginning you may pick up only a couple of words, if you practice daily, you will retain three, then four and so on. Within a few weeks, you will be able to repeat a surprising number of words after a mere glance at the page. Even when you feel you no longer need this exercise, it is important that you read aloud regularly. Read anything and read to anyone, anything, or no one—just read aloud.

- **Arm yourself with information.**
  There are a number of excellent books available devoted principally to the particular challenges of the audition. See the "Suggested Reading List" for some recommendations and don't go out on another reading until you have gleaned the wisdom from these excellent sources.

Let's face it: acting is an art defiant of logic. It comes from the soul and it is a slippery business. There are rules and they should be observed, but the rules alone will never make great acting.

William Redfield, *Letters from an Actor*

CHAPTER 20

A Thing Of The Spirit

Robert Edmond Jones, one of the most influential American set designers during the first half of the twentieth century, greatly admired actors. By his estimation, spending one's life as an actor was "to live as greatly as one can live."[1] I hope you will live "greatly" and never stop striving to be a better actor. No matter how long you study acting, you will never have all the answers. On the other hand, if you commit yourself to the work long enough, you will finally become a solid artisan, at least, and possibly an artist.

Every actor has heard the axiom: "This is show business—with the emphasis on *business*." They are wise words. When you are tending to the business part of acting, keep your feet firmly on the ground and your head out of the clouds. Nevertheless, when you are tending to the acting remember that, in spite of its frustrations, disappointments and all its down-to-earth considerations, the art of acting is occasionally noble. When you act, you set aside your own person so you are able to become the character. But, setting aside your person requires abandoning your protective devices and in so doing you reveal your innermost self. That collision of seemingly contradictory events results in the creation of a flesh and blood human—a human that you, and only you, could bring into being.

If you read Larry McMurtry's Pulitzer Prize winning novel, *Lonesome Dove,* a spot in your heart was permanently reserved for Gus McCrae. You finally put the book down feeling that Gus was someone you must have known in some shadow-life. If, however, you saw Robert Duvall's portrayal of that character in the television mini-series, your Gus could never be the same again. Because Duvall's illumination of that character added new dimensions to an already rich creation, now your Gus and mine are the same and there is a new Gus—not really different, but somehow more. What a gift good acting is to all of us and how indebted we are to those who work such magic.

A celebrated American actress giving her views on acting in 1917 said: "Great acting, of course, is a thing of the spirit."[2] An Irish poet advising the youth of Ireland said: "Keep in your souls some images of magnificence." [3] Whenever you act, I hope you will live by these words and make your work passionate, personal and principled. Be a generous actor. Invest your heart and soul extravagantly, refusing to withdraw from risk. Don't be an emotional miser and don't hide behind cardboard characters. Plunge pell-mell into that collision that results in the birth of the character. Shrink only from the temptation to hide your own true nature. Care not that your actions strip away the curtain that shields your innermost being from the skeptics. Celebrate the innermost you that is like no other and offer up that unique self as your special gift. My heart goes out to you knowing that so long as you act you must endure the emotional furnace that is the crucible of creation. May you never shrink from the flame. May your acting be a thing of your spirit.

FOOTNOTES

[1]Robert Edmond Jones, *The Dramatic Imagination*, pp. 32-33.
[2]Mrs. Minnie Maddern Fiske: *Her Views on Actors, Acting and the Problems of Productions; as told to Alexander Woollcott.* (New York: Century Company, 1917) pp. 76-89 passim. Copyright 1917. Quoted by Cole and Chinoy, p. 584.
[3]Robert Edmond Jones, p. 30.

Show me the books he loves and I shall know
The man far better than through mortal friends.

Silas Weir Mitchell,
Books and the Man. Stanza 1

Suggested Reading List

I have divided the books on the list into categories for easy reference but there are several that could have been listed in more than one category. I have placed an asterisk by the names of those that I consider essential. This list certainly doesn't include all the important acting books available—just some of my favorites. (Don't be discouraged by the publication dates listed here—I have taken this information from my personal library, collected over many years as you can see—these works are still in print.)

Books On The Craft Of Acting

*Brestoff, Richard. *The Camera Smart Actor*. Lyme, NH: Smith and Kraus, Inc., 1994.

*_____. *The Great Acting Teachers and Their Methods*. Lyme, NH: Smith and Kraus, Inc., 1995.

*Bruder, Melissa, Lee Michael Cohn, Madeleine Olnek, Nathaniel Pollack, Robert Previto, Scott Zigler. *A Practical Handbook For The Actor*. New York: Vintage Books, 1986.

Boleslavsky, Richard. *Acting: The First Six Lessons*. New York: Theatre Arts Books, 1956.

*Caine, Michael. *Acting In Film*. New York: Applause Theatre Book Publishers, 1990.

Cole, Toby and Helen Krich Chinoy, ed. *Actors On Acting*. New York: Crown Publishers, Inc., 1970.

Hagen, Uta. *Respect For Acting*. New York: Macmillan Publishing Co., Inc., 1973.

Hodge, Francis. *Play Directing*. Englewood Cliffs, N.J.: Prentice-Hall, Inc., 1971.

Lewis, Robert. *Method—Or Madness*. New York: Samuel French, Inc., 1958.

*McGaw, Charles. *Acting Is Believing*. New York: Holt, Rinehart and Winston, 1966.

Meisner, Sanford. *On Acting*. New York: Vintage Books, 1987.

Silverberg, Larry. *The Sanford Meisner Approach*. Lyme, NH: Smith and Kraus, Inc., 1994.

*Stanislavski, Constantin. *The Actor Prepares*. New York: Theatre Arts Books, 1973.

*_____. *Building A Character*. New York: Theatre Arts Books, 1971.

*_____. *Creating A Role*. New York: Theatre Arts Books, 1971.

*Shurtleff, Michael. *Audition*. New York: Walker and Company, 1978.

Books That Will Help You Learn To Concentrate

*Edwards, Betty. *Drawing On The Right Side Of The Brain*. Los Angeles: J. P. Tarcher, Inc., 1979.

*Gallwey, Timothy. *Inner Skiing*. New York: Bantam Books, Inc., 1981.

    (or any of the Gallwey books including *Inner Tennis, Inner Golf, Inner Game of Music*, etc.)

*LeShan, Lawrence. *How To Meditate*. New York: Bantam Books, Inc., 1975.

Books That Will Inspire You

Cameron, Julia. *The Artist's Way*. New York: The Putnam Publishing Group, 1992.

Jones, Robert Edmond. *The Dramatic Imagination*. New York: Theatre Arts Books, 1965.

May, Rollo. *The Courage To Create*. New York: Bantam Books, Inc., 1976.

Redfield, William. *Letters from an Actor*. New York: Limelight Editions, 1984.

Rilke, Rainer Maria. *Letters To A Young Poet*. New York: Vintage Books, 1986.

von Oech, Roger. *A Whack On The Side Of The Head*. New York: Warner Books, 1983.

Books On The Business End Of Acting

Callan, K. *How to Sell Yourself as an Actor*. Studio City, CA: Sweden Press, 1992.

Harmon, Renee. *How To Audition For Movies and TV*. New York: Walker and Company, 1992.

Hooks, Ed. *The Audition Book*. New York: Back Stage Books, 1989.

*Hunt, Gordon. *How To Audition*. Chicago: The Dramatic Publishing Company, 1977.

*Kerr, Judy. *Acting Is Everything*. Hollywood, CA: September Publishing, 1997.

Lewis, M. K. and Rosemary R. Lewis. *Your Film Acting Career*. Santa Monica, CA: Gorham House Publishing, 1989.

Mani, Karin. *The Working Actor's Guide*. Gardena, CA: Aaron Blake Publishers, 1997.

Index

Of Topics

Index Of Exercises
in Sequence

Index Of Exercises
by Title

We Would Appreciate Your Comments!

Thank you for purchasing *Let The Part Play You,* fourth edition. We sincerely hope you will find the book enjoyable and useful. Please let us know:

What do you like/dislike most about the book?

_____

_____

_____

_____

What are your favorite chapters?

_____   _____

_____   _____

If you are an actor, how has this book helped you hone your craft?

_____

_____

_____

If you are a teacher, how does this book help you?

_____

_____

_____

How were you introduced to the book?_____

How did you buy your copy of the book?

☐ Mail order   ☐ Bookstore   ☐ Other (specify)_____

Would you grant permission for us to use your name, title and comments in future advertising?
☐Yes   ☐No
                                 (please print)

Your Name_____

Address_____

City_____State_____Zip_____

Title _____

Signature_____

Please fold and tape this form so the address is visible, <u>attach postage</u> and mail us your comments.
Thank you!

From:

859 Hollywood Way, Suite 251
Burbank, CA 91505-2814

ORDER FORM

Please send the following books:
I understand that I may return the books for a full refund if I am not completely satisfied.

Send my copy/copies to:
     <u>PLEASE PRINT your full mailing address</u>:

NAME_____

INSTITUTION_____

ADDRESS_____
                                            (street)

_____
      (city)   (state)   (zip code)

LET THE PART PLAY YOU, fourth edition   _____copies @ $16.95 each
THE PLAYING IS THE THING   _____copies @ $16.95 each

Sales Tax: Please add 8.25% sales tax for orders shipped to a California address.

Shipping: $2.25 For the first book. Add 75 cents for each additional book.

Discounts are available for bulk orders.

Make your check or money order out to: **Wolf Creek Press**

Send your check or money order **along with this order form** to:

            Wolf Creek Press
            859 Hollywood Way, Suite 251
            Burbank, CA 91505-2814
            (Please do not send cash)

Please allow 4-6 weeks for delivery.
Thank you for your order.

WHAT OTHER PEOPLE ARE SAYING ABOUT THIS BOOK

"No actor should be without this excellent volume. For the beginner, Anita Jesse's superb book, *Let The Part Play You*, is one of the finest acting guides available. For the professional, her book is a joyous and inspirational reminder of how to keep our eyes and hearts on the target. Her wisdom is evident on every page and her clear-headed pragmatism is useful every day."
Richard Brestoff (Author of *The Camera Smart Actor*, faculty—University of Washington)

"Penetrates the mystique of acting without committing the crime of oversimplifying it. The opening chapter alone, "Freeing the Actor Within," is worth the price of admission!"
Al Guarino (Casting Director)

"absolutely wonderful ... a treasure." **Lou Ida Marsh** (Theatre Consultant)

"clear, insightful and full of practical ideas. This is magical support for the actor. I wouldn't want to be without it." **Rosemary Alexander** (Playwright/Director/Actor)

"An incredibly useful and entertaining book. *Let The Part Play You* clarifies so many of the mysteries in acting. An absolute must-read for all actors." **Lisa Wilcox** (Actor)

"a brilliant bare-bones approach to the craft of acting." **Leslie Jordan** (Actor)

"An intelligently crafted, loving tribute to both the actor and the craft. I couldn't endorse this more!" **Paulette Breen** (Television Producer)

"well thought-out ... many young actors will benefit from it." **Stacy Keach, Sr.** (Actor)

"concise arguments and intriguing exercises that have opened closed corridors in my own creativity. Unintentionally, Ms. Jesse has made me a better writer." **Jeff Andrus** (Screenwriter)

"a straightforward, personal approach ... openness and respect towards both the actor and the craft are on every page. I highly recommend it." **Randy Reinholz** (Faculty—Illinois State University)

"one of the clearest and most concise distillations of the actor's process that I have ever read. Anita Jesse by-passes all the usual jargon and goes right to the heart of the matter. *Let The Part Play You* should be in every actor's library."
Marilyn Allen Kearns (Teacher—The Actor's Workspace, North Carolina)

"Intelligent—Uncomplicated." **Jamie Farr** (Actor)

"Anita has such a personal touch that you feel as though you are right in the classroom with her when you read this book. You'll enjoy yourself."
Sandra Caruso (Author of *The Actor's Book of Improvisation*)

"*Let The Part Play You* enabled me to confidently prepare for my New York debut .... I will use the list of questions in Chapter 7 for every script I tackle the rest of my life! This book even makes the homework FUN."
Sandra Joseph (Actor)

About The Author

Anita Jesse established her studio in Los Angeles in 1978 and since then has coached hundreds of actors who work in film, television, and stage. She is one of the twenty-two coaches profiled in *The Actor's Guide to Qualified Acting Coaches, Los Angeles* by Larry Silverberg. Mr. Silverberg refers to these coaches as "some of our country's finest teachers."

The Anita Jesse Studio employs five professional actor-teachers who provide a broad range of training for the actor. In addition to technique classes for actors ranging in skill level from the working professional to the beginner, the studio provides specialized classes in acting for the camera, improvisation and commercial acting skills.

Anita's second book, *The Playing Is The Thing*, was published in 1996 by Wolf Creek Press. *Let The Part Play You* and *The Playing Is The Thing* are used by educators across the country. While Anita teaches at her studio in Los Angeles most of the year, she is invited to conduct professional and academic workshops across the country. She frequently appears as a guest lecturer at universities and university-sponsored seminars for actors and theatre educators.

Anita earned a Master of Fine Arts degree in Dramatic Production from the University of Texas at Austin and has been acting, teaching acting, and directing since then. Her work in film, television, and stage has earned her numerous awards including Best Actress, 1982, from the Christian Film Distributors' Association.

You can contact Anita through Wolf Creek Press (e-mail WlfCrkPrs@aol.com).